THE IDA MAE AND OSCAR TAYLOR BLACKBURN BOOKPLATE COLLECTION

7 00000 00330565

Selected Examples with Annotations
By Ivan Lee Weir and Natalie Alicia Weir

Acknowledgements

The authors wish to thank Marjorie Schlossman and her son, Herbert Ludwig Jr. for their generous support and technical help in creating this book, and in digitizing the over 3,200 images found in the Ida Mae and Oscar Taylor Blackburn Bookplate Collection.

Inquiries should be addressed to: ivanlweir@gmail.com

For

Doris Elaine Guptill Weir

Granddaughter of Ida Mae and Oscar Taylor Blackburn
Mother and Grandmother of the Authors

Thank you for all the stories you told about living with the Blackburns that led to writing about their lives and occupations and our discovery of their incredible world of bookplates.

TABLE OF CONTENTS

Introduction

In the fall of 1965 while attending the University of Oregon, I received a letter from Ms. Peterson in Minneapolis enquiring whether I would be interested in obtaining some of my great grandfather Blackburn's antiquarian books. Oscar Taylor Blackburn died in 1956, his estate passing first to his wife, Ida Mae who also died that year, and then to the Petersons who were the surviving relatives; Ms. Peterson was Ida Mae's sister. At the time she wrote, Lillian Peterson was in her late eighties.

"Yes," I said, "I'd love to have the Blackburn books." I had heard of Blackburn's antiquarian book and antique store from my mother who had lived in the Blackburn home when she was a young girl. As luck would have it, I was returning to Bemidji from Oregon via Minneapolis where Ms. Peterson lived later that month on my way to Afghanistan for two years. I arranged to visit Ms. Peterson, and with the help of my friend Richard Knutson, had the books boxed and sent to Bemidji.

As we were leaving, I noticed two shelves of small boxes, themselves about the size of a 9.5 x 6.5 x 1 inch book. I asked Ms. Peterson what they were. 'Oh, those are your great grandfather's bookplate collection', she said. "Do you want them?" "Why, yes", I replied, "I'd love to have them."

All in all, I was given forty-nine folios (a cardboard container with matted bookplates mounted one or more to a mat) and one additional box of loosely stored bookplates and other odd pamphlets, letters, etc. Each folio contained from a couple of dozen to over a hundred bookplates, many of them with dates from the late 1500s to the middle of the twentieth century. The bookplates had been designed and engraved by dozens of bookplate artists who lived and worked during those four centuries. In addition, the collection included several books and ten *Year Books* published by the American Society of Bookplate Collectors and Designers. Oscar Taylor Blackburn was a member of the Society since its inception.

The folios were stored in two large cardboard boxes for the next fifty years, carried from one state to another through a number of rented and owned houses that variously were burned, robbed, vandalized and located in high risk areas. Largely ignored until the spring of 2014, a happy circumstance allowed me to begin work on cataloging the book plate collection at the Marjorie Schlossman Art Studio in Fargo, North Dakota. With major help from Herb Ludwig, Jr. a system of organizing, cataloging, digitizing and electronically storing the 3,267 bookplates was executed. Neither the internet nor desktop publishing had been invented in 1965, but with the technology available in 2014, we were able to scan and digitize the whole collection.

Ida Mae and Oscar Taylor Blackburn spent years identifying, collecting, trading, and organizing bookplates in conjunction with their engraving, bookstore and antique businesses. Thus, ninety percent of the collection and conservation work had already been performed by the Blackburn's, not to mention the hundreds of hours invested by artists, designers, engravers and printers in creating those bookplates.

A small number of the bookplates have been selected for inclusion in this book. No systematic attempt was made to represent all or even the most important engravers. Natalie and I selected those plates that were most appealing to us at the time and that we thought might be interesting to others. Having gone through the entire collection several times, we are proud to acknowledge that our ancestors, Ida Mae and Oscar Taylor Blackburn, created an amazing collection of bookplates.

The story of bookplates is also the story of books, libraries and collections, and a story of family, legacy and heritage. Our story began in 1066 when a knight who was part of the Norman conquest of England was awarded a piece of land by William the Conqueror…

Chapter I: The Ghost Engraver

Oscar Taylor Blackburn was born on June 23 (1863-1956) to John Taylor Blackburn (1841—1919) and Jane Virginia Taylor (aka Sarah Jane) (1843—1876) in Ackworth (near Pontefract), England. After Virginia died, the father and son and two daughters immigrated to the United States in 1881 when Oscar was 18 years old.

Prior to leaving England, Oscar apprenticed at age 14 to a watchmaker, and family lore (word of mouth from his granddaughter Leila) has it that at one time he was employed with maintenance of "Big Ben" in London. During Oscar's years as a watch repairman, watches and clocks were all mechanical, highly intricate, and precise. He opened a watch repair shop in Minneapolis when he was 80 years old after having been an engraver of silver and bookplates for most of his life.

Oscar married **Ida Mae Wineberg** (1867—1956) and according to his other granddaughter Elaine, Ida Mae was from the South. The Weinberg family emigrated from Germany in 1842, and the early ancestors lived in Doddridge County, Virginia (which later became West Virginia). Oscar met and married Ida Mae in Salina, Kansas. Based on genealogical research, we learned Ida Mae's ancestors immigrated from Syke, Germany to Doddridge County, in 1842 on the ship *Vesta*.

Ida Mae Wineberg Blackburn
Photo courtesy of Scott Brockelman

Early members of the Wineberg family moved to Kansas in the 1870s. The Blackburn's had two daughters, Doris (1890—1981) and Lillian (1895—1956), and a child John (1912—1912) who died in his first year. Ida and Oscar were married for 68 years, and died in the same year, as did Lillian Peterson who lived with Ida and Oscar in the last years of her life. Lillian was survived by her husband's sister who gave the bookplates to us.

Besides bookplate engraving, the Blackburn's owned an antiquarian book and antique store in Minneapolis that traded in collectable books, music and other sought after objects such as Tiffany lamps, oriental carvings, etc.

Oscar Taylor Blackburn
Engraver Oscar Taylor Blackburn
(Plate 17010)

Oscar joined the American Bookplate Society in 1913, the year that it was founded. His friend, H.E. MacDonald, who wrote a biographical sketch of Oscar Taylor Blackburn for the *1933 Yearbook of the American Society of Bookplate Collectors and Designers*, said "… bookplates have played a minor role in Blackburn's varied experiences in engraving…", the observation being that Blackburn spent much of his engraving time adorning watches, jewelry, and other objects. About 1910 his firm assigned him to engraving full time, and he advanced his knowledge and experience in bookplates by collecting and studying those of the accepted masters.

H. E. MacDonald observed that Blackburn did not sign many of his bookplates but by choice and necessity worked as a "ghost engraver".

Oscar Taylor Blackburn
"The Ghost Engraver"
(Plate 17009)

Between 1910 and 1933 Oscar Taylor Blackburn engraved 64 plates, and during the remainder of his life that many more as he was still engraving until two years before his death. The Bookplates of Minnesota plate described below was engraved in 1954 to advertise an exhibition held of bookplates at the Minneapolis Library.

In addition to engraving, Blackburn played the violin with a Minneapolis symphony (it was thought that this symphony was the Minneapolis Symphony, but we were unable to verify this fact through a call to the Symphony historian); his violin is still in possession of one of his great grandchildren.

Occasionally, Oscar would write articles about engraving. Following is an article he wrote for the *Engravers Bulletin* in 1942.

<h1 style="text-align:center">"There Were Dragons in Those Days"</h1>
by
Oscar Taylor Blackburn

There Were Dragons in Those Days
Engraver Oscar Taylor Blackburn
(Plate 17036)

The story of Saint George, patron saint of England, like most ancient tales appears to be a mixture of fact and fancy. That he really existed is not doubted; the birthplace is variously given as Armorica in Gaul (now Brittany) and as Cappadocia in Asia Minor. He was a Christian and was beheaded April 23, 303 A.D. in the great persecution by Emperor Diocletian, and was buried at Lydda in Palestine. His selection as patron saint dates from soon after the Norman Conquest and in 1222 the National Synod at Oxford decreed that the anniversary of his death should be observed as a festival.

Saint George and the Dragon have always figured largely in English Heraldry. The dragon was the standard of English kings since the Conquest, was borne at the battle of Crecy and as a badge by Henry VII and Richard III, but was never a charge on the royal coat-of-arms. The arms of London display dragons as supporters, and a figure of Saint George on horseback spearing the dragon, and suspended from a collar of roses is the insignia of the Knights of the Garter. The star of the order has the Cross of Saint George, red on a silver ground, surrounded by the garter with the inscription "Honi soit qui mal y pense". [Evil unto him who thinks evil of it.—Wikipedia]

It seems appropriate that several of the [holders of the] name of Saint George should have made the science of heraldry their life's work. Sir Henry Saint George (1581—1644) was Norroy and Garter King of Arms; his two sons, Sir Thomas and Sir Henry, were later Kings of Arms as also was Sir Richard who died in 1635.

The "Golden Legend" (1507) says in part: "This holy martyr Saynt George is patrone of this realme of England in ye worship of whome is founded ye noble order of a garter; and also ye noble college in ye Castell of Windsor, which college is nobly endowed to honor and worshyppe almighty God and his bless martyr Saynt George."

Johnson's "Seven Champions of Christendom" (1597) and Percy's "Reliques" coincide in romantic accounts of Saint George, which state he was born at Coventry, the son of Lord Albert. His mother died at his birth and the infant was stolen by a witch who raised him to be a soldier. In manhood after much travel and many knightly adventures, he found the Princess Sabra about to be sacrificed to a dragon, slew the dragon, rescued the princess and brought her to England. Later they were married and lived happily ever after at Coventry. This must have been a later Saint George as the scenes seem to have been laid at the time of the crusades.

A bare place is shown where nothing will grow on Dragon's Hill in Berkshire and it is said Saint George killed a dragon there. The slaying of the dragon by Saint George may be said to typify the triumph of the Christian over the forces of evil, and we live in hope and confidence that the banner of Saint George carried against ruthless aggression will ultimately triumph.
"There are Dragons in these days."

St. George slaying the dragon appears in several bookplates, including that of Winston Churchill (Plate 36035), as well as one engraved by Thomas W. Nason in a bookplate for Samuel Robert Morrill (Plate 10077). Blackburn used the Saint Christopher theme in his bookplate for Jack and Jerry Haines (Plate 39032).

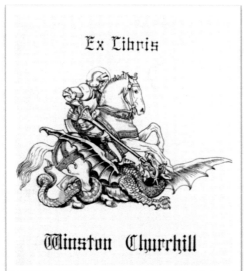

Winston Churchill
Engraver Unknown "Saint George Slaying the Dragon"
(Plate 36035)

Winston Churchill (1874—1965) was England's Prime Minister during World War II. He had been a war correspondent, an officer in the British Army, and a politician who held several offices before becoming the Prime Minister. Churchill was from the Marlborough lineage. He won a Nobel Prize for Literature (1953) for his history of the Second World War and other books, and was the first person to be made an honorary citizen of the United States. His mother was an American citizen.

An *Engraver's Bulletin* editor's note to the "Dragons" story indicates that Oscar Taylor Blackburn engraved another plate besides the Haines plate showing St. George slaying the dragon, included here as plate 17036.

Samuel Robert Morrill bookplate
Engraver Thomas Nason
(Plate 10077)

Thomas W. Nason (1889—1971) is a highly collected book plate engraver who specialized in wood block prints. Besides engraving, he produced artistic renderings of New England countryside and included animals, plants and early American structures in his prints. Some refer to him as the "poet engraver of New England". Besides 22 bookplates between 1922 and 1937, he did etchings and illustrations. His work is found in dozens of American and European museums, and over his career he won several prestigious prizes for art. Samuel Robert Morrill and his son were dealers in rare books.

The Jack and Jerry Haines image engraved by Oscar Taylor Blackburn shows a knight on a charger although not slaying a dragon. Not many of Blackburn's plates were printed on colored paper.

Jack and Jerry Haines
Engraver Oscar Taylor Blackburn
(Plate 39032)

George Allen's (1832—1907) Ruskin House (Plate 41037) was a publishing company in London. At the end of the 19th century Ruskin House published the novels of Jane Austen. The engraver is unidentified, but as George Allen was an engraver, he may have done his own plate. The publishing house was famous for printing antiquarian books. George Allen once worked for 79 days on a door that John Ruskin showed a model of as a representative example of fine English craftsmanship.

John Ruskin (1819—1900) was a British art critic, lecturer, writer and essayist, and painter of whom it was said 'could out-paint most painters' he critiqued. Ruskin was a widely influential social critic whose ideas anticipated the environmental movement of the late 20th century. Among his many accomplishments, he founded *The Guild of St. George*, a utopian living experiment dedicated to the common man that exists today as a charitable organization.

George Allen's Ruskin House
Engraver George Allen
(Plate 41037)

William K. Montague by Oscar Taylor Blackburn with the inscription After Aubrey Beardsley (Plate 17011)
and John Lumsden by Aubrey Beardsley (Plate 09002)

Oscar Taylor Blackburn created a bookplate for William K. Montague styled after the art of Aubrey Beardsley (Plate 17011). The similarity can be seen from the visual comparison to the John Lumsden plate sculpted by **Aubrey Beardsley** (1872—1898) (Plate 09002).

BFC Book of Wells
Engraver *Oscar Taylor Blackburn*
(Plate 17017)

Two of Blackburn's more elaborate designs are found in Ye Booke of Wells (Plate 17017), and in the Eleanor White and James Bradshaw Mintener plate that shows their coat-of-arms (Plate 17004).

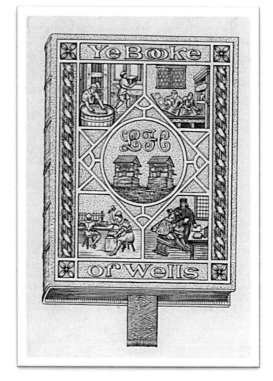

8

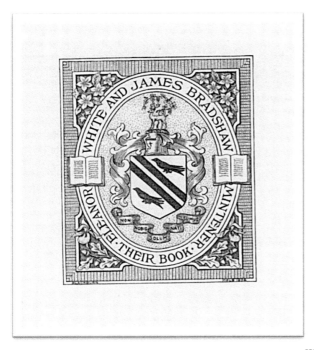

Eleanor White and James Bradshaw Mintener
Engraver Oscar Taylor Blackburn
(Plate 17004)

In 1954, Oscar Taylor Blackburn compiled and arranged a show of Bookplates of Minnesota at the Minneapolis Public Library. Plates were selected from two folios of Minnesota bookplates containing 253 items including about 40 bookplates of his design. For the Library show, he engraved the copper plate below.

When writing is included on the plate, a reverse image must be engraved in order for it to appear correctly on the print. An example of a copper plate that was engraved with a reverse image is the Blackburn "Bookplates of Minnesota" copper plate engraving. Notice that the lettering is what would be seen if the printed plate was held up to a mirror.

Bookplates of Minnesota
Engraver Oscar Taylor Blackburn
(Plate 50201)

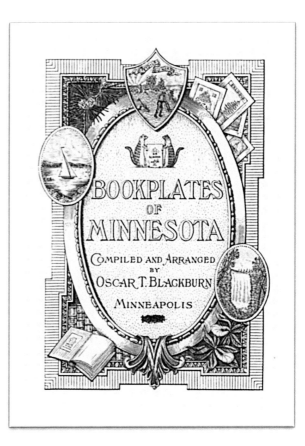

In a very thorough book on the genealogy of Blackburns in America, **Evelyn D. (Blackburn) Gibson** wrote that "Blackburn" is registered by the College of Heralds to **Gilbert Blackburn** of Hale Hall, Lancaster, Lord of the Manor of Hale. She also observed that the helmet in the coat-of-arms is indicative of the Blackburn decendancy from a Norman knight, and other evidence is set forth in *William Alexander Abram's book, Blackburn, the Decent of the Manor; the de Blackburn Family, 1877.*

The name Blackburn may have come from Old English 'bloec' meaning black and 'burna' meaning stream. A stream runs through the hamlet of Blackburn. Through Ancestry.com, Blackburn ancestors were traced back to 1645 in Ryton, Yorkshire, England.

Other narratives speak of the town of Blackburn as early as 1066, originating as a bequeath by William the Conqueror. Records indicate the presence in England of Willelmus de Blakburn from Yorkshire in 1379. Blackburn Manor consisted of a castle and 10,000 thousand acres, and was awarded to a Norman knight (French) in 1066 at the time of the Normal Conquest for service of accompanying William the Conqueror during the Battle of Hastings. The village became Blackburn, England that continues to this day.

Interesting and reoccurring stories concern a wild boar that was killed by one of the knights who accompanied William the Conqueror to England in 1066. One story has it that a knight by the name of Blakburn killed the boar because it was terrorizing the people in the area, and that William awarded possession of the settlement and 4,000 acres, all of which became the town of Blackburn and Blackburn Manor.

Blackburn
Engraver Oscar Taylor Blackburn
(Plate 17005)

A similar story originating about the same time concerns a legend of The Wild Boar of Westmoreland. In the reign of King John (1199—1216), a wild boar inhabited the forest between Kendal and Windermere, ravaging and killing pilgrims on their way to worship in the Chapel of the Blessed Virgin on St. Mary's Isle on Windermere. Villagers and pilgrims were terrorized, many not returning having been devoured by the monster along the way. Something had to be done.

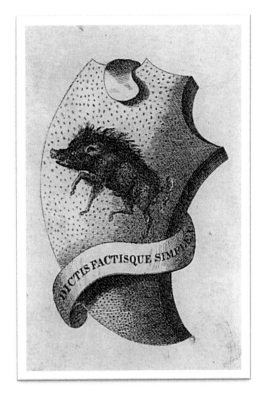

One **Richard de Gylpyn aka Alexander Lewius Peace** (cir. 1066) who was a secretary to William the Conqueror found the monster, had a ferocious battle with it, and slew it on the banks of a little stream now known as the Gilpin. After his return to France, his fame grew, and the Baron of Kendal awarded him a lordship of the Manor of Kentmere. He changed his family crest to that of a black boar on a gold background, with the inscription Dictus Factus Simplex—'honest in word and deed'.

Exactly who commissioned the bookplate is unknown. The estate was increased during Elizabethan times, and was in the Gilpin family for 12 generations, but was destroyed by Cromwell's troops during the English Civil War.

An older Oscar Taylor Blackburn (cir. 1955) appears in the following photograph, possibly the last in his lifetime. His friend, H. E. MacDonald, described him as a gentleman who was "a charming correspondent who had a vital interest in the various social and intellectual usages that go to make up the amenities of existence", an observation borne out by his several interests and accomplishments. Oscar Taylor Blackburn emigrated from England to the United States in the late 1800s, but other persons having the Blackburn name arrived on the North American continent before the Revolutionary war.

Documentary evidence of other Blackburn lineage in America begins with John Blackburn, Sr. (1675) and Mary Courtney (1680). Andrew Blackburn arrived in Georgia in 1751, Richard Blackburn arrived in Virginia in 1757, and Benjamin Blackburn arrived in Bermuda in 1774. Thomas Blackburn landed in New York in 1846, and W. Blackburn arrived in San Francisco in 1851 as did two other persons with the Blackburn name. Evelyn Gibson published a book titled *Blackburn and Allied Descendants of John Blackburn, Sr. Who Came from Ireland to Pennsylvania in 1736*; Ireland was a departure point for immigrants coming to the new world as well as a place where many of the Blackburn clan lived.

The early Blackburn's in America were Quakers as were their Irish ancestors, although Gibson reports a Blackburn served in George Washington's army and another fought in the American Civil War. These Blackburn's may not have been directly related to Oscar Taylor Blackburn who came from England much later in 1881.

In his short biographical sketch of Oscar Taylor Blackburn for the 1933 *Yearbook*, H. E. MacDonald wrote,

> "Back in merry old England in 1649 at Pontefract, when the castle finally surrendered to Cromwell's forces, six of the defenders were exempted from the general amnesty extended to the garrison. These six had shown too stubborn

resistance and too persistent activity to be included in the general pardon. One of these was a Michael Blackburn. It is pleasant to imagine that this persistent determination may be a family trait that helped our present bearer of the name teach himself the art of engraving" (*Year Book* 1933:p. 33).

Oscar Taylor Blackburn
Photo Cir. 1955
(Plate 17022)

Michael Blackburne (d. 1649) actually was a Royalist defender of Pontefract Castle being besieged by Oliver Cromwell's forces in 1648-1649. After eight months of attacks and negotiations, Colonel John Morris and Coronet Michael Blackburne managed to escape only to be captured ten days later. As MacDonald said, Morris, Blackburne and four others were exempted from the general amnesty accorded the Royalist defenders at Pontefract Castle and instead condemned for being 'guilty of other notorious and bloody crimes', one assertion being that Morris had 'hanged a gentlewoman only because she looked like an Irish lady.' Morris denied guilt of his crimes on the gallows, but Blackburne refused to speak more, saying "he that has spoken so much cannot be heard". After another attempt at escape, they were put in Tyburn prison and soon executed.

Other than the observation that Oscar Taylor Blackburn had an apprenticeship in watchmaking, there is little record of his education. He read widely, and by his own statement was self-taught in engraving. His bookplate engraving was a sideline to engraving on silver and timepieces for a company in Minneapolis. Late in life, he started his own watch repair and engraving company.

St. Giles Church at Pontefract,
England
(Plate 50117)

The Blackburn—Weir Family Genealogy

William Blackburn 1645—b. Ryton, Shropshire, England
Luke Blackburn 1672—1728 b. Durham, Durham, England
John Blackburn 1704—b. Ryton, Shropshire, England
John Blackburn 1741—1748 (?) b. Alendale, Northumberland, England
John Blackburn 1786—1861 b. Yorkshire, England
John Marcus Blackburn 1808—1878 b. Ackworth, Yorkshire, England
John Taylor Blackburn 1841—1919 b. Pontefract, West Riding, England.
Oscar Taylor Blackburn b. 1863—1956 b. Yorkshire, England
Doris Ada Blackburn Guptill 1890--1981 b. Kansas, USA
Doris Elaine Guptill Weir 1917—Present b. Minneapolis, Minnesota
Elaine Weir is the grandmother of Natalie and the mother of Ivan Weir.

The Guptill side of the family, beginning with the marriage of Doris Blackburn, daughter of Oscar and Ida Mae, to Lee Guptill, can be traced back to the Winthrop Expedition of 1630 that arrived in North America with 11 ships; a Guptill ancestor was on board of one of the ships. Although related by marriage to the Bernhardson-Nelson Swedish immigrants of Comstock, North Dakota, the Weir line originated in Scotland and began life in the United States in a little Minnesota town called Wolverton. Both sides of the Blackburn—Guptill--Weir family came from England.

Thomas Blackburne, Esq. of Hale near Warrington, Lancashire
Engraver Unknown
(Plate 40023)

Thomas Blackburne was a wealthy Cheshire salt merchant whose estate included Orford Hall in Orford, Warrington, England. His son, **John Blackburne** (1646—1724), High Sherriff of Lancashire, made major improvements to the house that was originally built in 1232. John's son, also named John Blackburne (1694—1786), was a naturalist and horticulturalist who brought a collection of rare plants, trees and unusual animals to the estate. He and his daughter, Anna, a noted botanist herself, were the first in the England to grow pineapples, coffee, tea and sugar cane in a hothouse, and they also cultivated citrus fruits.

There are five John Blackburn's shown in the genealogy chart above, the most recent being Oscar Taylor Blackburn's father. Whether the bookplate on the left belongs to one of them is unknown.

The Blackburn Collection also contains eight bookplates for persons who share the Blackburn name and may be Oscar Taylor Blackburn ancestors. Albeit some of the relationships are indirect, the Blackburn name has been present during most of English and American history.

W. Blackburne
Engraver Unknown
(Plate 40024)

Hale Hall (or Manor) came into the Blackburne family through the marriage of Thomas Blackburne to Ireland Green of Childwall in 1752, and passed to their son, John Blackburne who was born in 1754, became High Sheriff in 1781, and represented Lancashire as a Tory in Parliament from 1784 to 1830. Upon his death in 1833, a son John Ireland Blackburne inherited Hale Hall, as did his son also named John Ireland.

John Blackburn Esq. of Hale
Engraver Unknown
(Plate 40022)

The lettering at the upper border of the shield reads **John Blackburn Esq. of Hale** (Plate 40022). According to British History Online Hale Hall was still owned by Blackburne descendants as late as 1907. The estate was gifted to Warrington Council by **Colonel Robert Ireland Blackburne** in 1916 to be turned into a War Memorial. The house no longer stands.

An interesting bookplate design development is the figure of a semi-nude woman holding the Blackburn shield in Plate 40022. This may be a picture of either Anne Rodbard who married John Blackburne—a Member of Parliament for 46 years-- or her cousin Sarah Rodbard, all three of whom were painted by an artist of the time named **George Romney** (1734—1802).

Or, the model may have been Lady Emma Hamilton, a patron of Romney's, who was for a long time the mistress of Lord Horatio Nelson. Romney did over 60 portraits of Lady Hamilton. Romney's paintings often included very attractive women, not unusual for a short period of time just preceding the Victorian Age of stodginess. Romney became famous, rivaling Gainsborough in popularity. His paintings are exhibited in several dozen British and American museums. George Romney was an ancestor of a current American presidential aspirant of the same name.

Andrew Blackburn
Engraver Unknown
(Plate 40026)

Except for the Andrew Blackburn plate, all of the shields contain an image of two stars above a serrated band with one star beneath. Oscar Taylor Blackburn included this motif in his heraldic plate (Plate 17005), and this is the motif used by the town of Blackburn, England on its name plate.

Bibliotheca Elizabethana
apud Blackburn in Com: Lane:
(Plate 40025)

The purpose of the Elizabethana bookplate is unclear; it appears to be a plate for Bibliotheca Elizabethana which was a publication concerning the theater of the Royal Irish Academy.

A lengthy description of the origins of this coat of arms is given in Evelyn D. Gibson's book, *Blackburn and Allied Descendants of John Blackburn, Sr.,* who came from Ireland to Pennsylvania in 1736.

There are many Blackburns and Blackburn descendants in the United States who are not directly related to Oscar Taylor Blackburn although further research may find a more direct lineage than is presented here.

Wm. Blackburne M.D.
Engraver Unknown
(Plate 40028)

The plate for **Wm. Blackburne M. D.** has the same heraldic characteristics of the other Blackburne plates without the helmet or other body armor. The implication is that the Blackburne's have hung up their shield and pursued other endeavors, such as medicine. The inclusion of the symbolic broken tree and the small structures on the hills in the background anticipates the artistic designs that began to appear in bookplates in the 1920s.

16

Wᴹ BLACKBURNE M.D.

Chapter II: British Antiquarian Bookplates

Examination of the British bookplates in the Blackburn Collection involves an exploration of British history. Early English bookplates were designed and engraved at the beginning of the 16th century. Blackburn's British folios include bookplates of Kings and Queens, Prime Ministers and Ambassadors, Lords and Ladies, other Nobility, authors and explorers. Some of them are presented below with short narratives about their owners or engravers.

Ambrose Holbech of Mollington
Engraver Unknown
(Plate 18050)

One of the older English bookplates in the Collection was made for **Mr. Ambrose Holbech of Mollington the elder** (1596—1662), and his son **Ambrose Holbech of Mollington the younger,** (d. about 1705) and his descendants, dated 1702 (Plate 18050). Holbech's were a long standing English family who purchased the Manor of Mollington in the first half of the 17th century. Ambrose Holbech the Younger gave 50 pounds to be invested for the poor, and his father had previously donated funds to help poor people of the region.

Mollington is a very old agricultural parish dating back to the early years of the 11th century and persisting into the 20th century. Mollington Manor was held by the Holbech's until 1950 when the Holbech estates were broken up and sold mostly to tenants.

Various manors and estates and documents of county government are documented in *British History Online, 'Parishes Mollington,' A History of the County of Oxford: Volume 10: Banbury hundred, 1972* which also includes a very thorough history of the area.

William Norcliffe of the Inner Temple
London
Engraver Unknown
(Plate 18052)

The Inner Temple derives from the Knights Templar, and had its beginnings in the 1154—1189 reign of Henry II. The 'inn of Templar' was actually a place where professional legal people—judges and lawyers—met. **William Norcliffe (**d. 1735) had legal training at the Inner Temple and practiced in London. His plate is dated 1703.

The Manor of Loxley, located about 3 miles from Stratford, came into the Norcliffe family by William's marriage to Jane Miller who had inherited it from a long line of Miller's. One of the Manor's owners had been the second cousin of Thomas Nash of Stratford who was married to Shakespeare's granddaughter, Elizabeth Hall.

Gostlet Harington of Marshfield
in the County of Gloucester Gent
Engraver Unknown (Plate 18051)

The town of Marshfield was occupied first by the Loyalists during the Civil war (1643) and later by Cromwell's forces (1648) when Michael Blackburn lost his life at Pontefract. The Battle of Lansdowne was fought at Marshfield. The poem, "The Highwayman", by Alfred Noyes, takes place in the Marshfield area: "The highwayman came riding, riding up to the old inn door…" The engravers are unknown, but the styles of the Norcliffe and Gostlet bookplates are highly similar.

18

William Fitzroy Duke of Cleveland

Gostlet Harginton's (1682—1706) plate is dated 1706. John Harrington and Mary Gostlet built Tolzey or Town House for the town of Marshfield in 1690. At various times, it housed the city government, jail and fire engine. Bronze and stone age implements were discovered about ½ mile away, and a skeleton in a stone casket was uncovered.

William Fitzroy, 3rd Duke of Cleveland
Engraver Unknown
(Plate 18132)

The 2nd Duke of Cleveland, The father of **William Fitzroy 3rd Duke of Cleveland** (1698—1774), was the illegitimate son of King Charles II of England, Scotland, and Ireland. Charles was overthrown, and later had his head forcibly removed from his body. Both William's father and William did quite well, living off sinecures provided by the Crown even after the demise of King Charles. William's dukedom became extinct after his death as he had no children. It was revived many years later for a later ancestor.

Bruce of Ampthill
Engraver Unknown
(Plate 41060)

The plate for The **Right Honorable Charles Viscount Bruce of Ampthill** (1682—1747) is dated 1712. Bruce's mother, Mary Somerset, was a noted early botanist.

The title, "The Right Honorable..." was used in the United Kingdom as a personal honorific for earls, viscounts, barons and their wives, and as an official designation for some offices, for example, the Right Honorable Lord Mayor of London. Bruce was married three times, lastly to Lady Caroline Campbell when she was 18 years old and he was 47. He was a member of the British nobility, as were his wives

Sir Thomas Hanmer of Hanmer
Engraver Unknown
(Plate 41063)

Sir Thomas Hanmer (1677—1746) of the 4th Baronet was the speaker of Westminster in Oxford, and during his career was received in great state by Louis XIV in Paris.

As a politician, Sir Thomas Hanmer took ambiguous stands that raised the ire of his contemporaries. Horace Walpole, leading the opposition party, attacked Hanmer's politics and apparent lack of virility. Walpole the Elder wrote "He had a very handsome mien and appearance, but tis said he could not please the ladies", and Walpole the Younger said he was "a dainty Speaker, who was first married to the Dowager Dutchess of Grafton, and afterwards espousing a young lady, the first night he made some faint efforts toward consummation, and then begged her pardon for her disappointment..." His pursuits also included being a Shakespeare scholar and publisher.

Deburgh Earl of Clanricarde
Engraver Unknown
(Plate 41054)

The plate for John Tomas **Deburgh Earl of Clanricarde (**1744—1808) is one of the earlier bookplates showing the identity of the engraver on the bottom edge of the plate, **W. Hibbart**. This plate is included in Henry W. Fincham's *British and American Book Plates, 1927*. The plate is dated 1750.

The Irish Earldom of Clanricarde was created in 1543 when the first Earl of Clanricarde was awarded the baronetcy by Henry VIII, King of Ireland, Scotland and England. The de Burgh name may not have appeared until Richard de Burgh (1572—1635) who was the 4th Earl of Clanricarde, and served Queen Elizabeth I against the Irish and their Spanish sympathizers.

Dashwood, Lord Le Despencer
Engraver Unknown
(Plate 41051)

Francis Dashwood, Lord Despencer (1708—1782) was from a long line of Despencer's, the title originating in 1385 about the time of Edward the Black Prince. He was named the Black Prince by the French because he wore black armor. Dashwood was the Prince of Wales and Duke of Cornwall and the father of King Richard II of England. His wife was called 'the fair maid of Kent'.

Francis Dashwood was the 15th Lord Despencer. He was a member of the royalty, served in the British Parliament under Walpole the Younger, and was a jokester and rake. He helped establish and patronized a 'men's club' in London called the Hellfire Club, a place where persons of quality could go to take part in immoral activities. One of the members of the Hellfire Club was the painter and engraver, William Hogarth, who did a portrait of Dashwood.

William Hogarth, Engraver
Engraver William Hogarth
(Plate 12006)

An early English engraver highly recognized in the art world was **William Hogarth** (1697—1764) whose plate is dated 1720. Hogarth worked as a painter and print engraver and is known for developing 'series' prints such as 'A Harlot's Progress' and 'Marriage a la mode' (Wiki/William Hogarth). He became Sergeant Painter to the Monarchy in 1757 until his death in 1764.

Lord Archibald Campbell (cir.1563) was a Scottish nobleman, businessman, politician, lawyer and soldier. He was the son of Archibald Campbell, the 10th Earl and 1st Duke of Argyll. His titles included 3rd Duke of Argyll, 1st Earl of Ilay, and Lord High Treasurer of Scotland under Queen Anne. Campbell was one of the founders of the Royal Bank of Scotland. One of Campbell's descendants was Jenny von Westphalen, the wife of Karl Marx. As he had no male successors, when he died he left his English property to his mistress, Ann Williams. The bookplate attributed to him may be for a relative of another generation, but the design includes elements belonging to the Campbell lineage.

The **5th Earl of Argyle, Lord Archibald Campbell**, was born in Scotland in 1532. His contemporaries included William Shakespeare (1564—1616), Queen Elizabeth I (1533—1603) who was the daughter of Ann Boleyn and Henry VIII, and Mary (Stuart) Queen of Scots (1542—1587). Mary Queen of Scots became queen when she was 6 days old and was a cousin of Queen Elizabeth I. Elizabeth was Queen when Mary was executed but denied responsibility for the execution saying her Privy Council had acted against her orders.

Lord Campbell was a politician who aligned himself both for and against Mary Queen of Scots. He led a movement against her that contributed to her capture and imprisonment, but he was with her during her reign a Queen of Scotland. Lord Campbell became the Lord Chancellor of Scotland in 1572, a year before his own death. Mary was beheaded by Queen Elizabeth I; among the charges against her was adultery and murder.

Walter Raleigh, a divine or priest, (1586—1646) was the son of Sir Walter Raleigh's brother, Sir Carew Raleigh. Walter Raleigh took holy orders, and became Chaplin to William Herbert, 3rd Earl of Pembroke. He was murdered in his church, attempting to keep a letter to his wife from the wrong eyes. His career, however, was wildly eclipsed by his more famous uncle.

Sir Walter Raleigh (1554—1618), was knighted by Queen Elizabeth in 1585, and was an aristocrat, writer, poet, soldier, politician, courtier, spy, and was rumored to have been a lover of the Queen herself. When he secretly married without the Queen's permission, he and his wife were sent to the Tower of London for a period of time, apparently living together as one of their son's was born during their incarceration. He was let out in 1616, and began a search for El Dorado.

He didn't find El Dorado, but Raleigh managed to enrage the Spanish ambassador who demanded his arrest, imprisonment, and execution. Upon seeing the ax to be used for his beheading, he said "This is a sharp Medicine, but it is a Physician for all diseases and miseries."

Lord Napier
Engraver Unknown
(Plate 36013)

The first Lord Napier was awarded the baronetcy in 1627; the baronetcy survives to this day. Its family seat is the Thirlestane Castle, near Ettrick in Scotland. **John Napier** (1550—1670) is credited with the invention of logarithms in 1614.

The bookplate is that of the 9th Lord Napier but there is some ambiguity as to whether it is that of the first Lord Napier and **9th Laird Napier of Murchiston** (1576—1645) or a later Lord Napier of the 19th century who was instrumental in early trade with China. Nevertheless, the coat of arms shown in the center of the plate is of Napier.

The death of Queen Elizabeth in 1603 marked the end of the Stuart rule of Great Britain. Lord Napier accompanied King James VI, the first of the Stewarts, to London; Napier was later imprisoned for supposed impropriety with royal funds, although he was later absolved of the crime. Several generations of Napier's have continued their involvement in British government.

King George I
Engraver J. Pine
(Plate 36041)

King James VI was the sixth king of England and first king of Scotland who ruled until 1625. He was succeeded by Charles I who was overthrown by Cromwell in 1649, the final battle occurring in Pontefract where Michael Blackburn 1649 was granted a stubborn but honorable death. After being tried for treason, Charles I was beheaded and England had its only period of modern history not under royal rule.

In 1714, the House of Hanover began its rule of England with **King George I** (1660—1727) whose bookplate is above. George I ruled from 1714 to 1727. George I spoke French and German but only a little English. His reign was fraught with turmoil, and besides not getting along with his son, George II, he once put his own wife in prison.

Thomas Fytton Armstrong
Engraver Unknown
(Plate 26053)

Lieutenant-Colonel **Thomas Fytton Armstrong** (1624—1684) was a captain in the Royal Horse Guards, became a Member of Parliament in 1660, and served in King Charles II army.

He was wrongly accused of participation in the Rye House Plot and sentenced to death by Judge Jeffries, who found him guilty for outlawry and high treason. After his execution at Tyburn prison, Armstrong's widow and daughter petitioned the government to restore the 12,000 pounds that were confiscated from Armstrong's estate that left them in 'a state of want and misery'. Armstrong was exonerated by history, but whether his funds were returned is unknown.

Lord Henry Grey, 11th Duke of Kent
Engraver Unknown
(Plate 36017)

Also present at that time **was Henry (Grey), the Eleventh Duke of Kent** (1664—1740) who was the last of the Kent line. He was the 11th Earl of Kent and installed as a knight of the garter. Under King George I, Grey was the Lord Steward of the Household, Lord Privy Seal, and one of the Lord Justices.

King George I was followed by King George II whose term on the throne was from 1727 to 1760. Under George II, the British Empire expanded into India with Clive's victory at Arcot in 1751, and Wolfe's capture of French held Quebec which transferred Canada to British rule. At that time, the American colonies were already under British rule.

Sir Robert Walpole
England's First Prime Minister
Engraver Unknown
(Plate 36010)

Sir Robert Walpole (1676—1745) became England's acting first Prime Minister, and served both King George I and King George II. During his career, Walpole was impeached and spent six months in the Tower of London but was released and later returned to government. In 1735, King George II made Robert Walpole a present of 10 Downing Street, a location that is still the official residence of the Prime Minister of England.

A trade dispute was elevated into the War of Jenkin's Ear with Spain in 1739, so named after Robert Jenkins had his ear cut off by the Spanish Guard in 1731 as punishment for raiding Spanish ships. The war took place in what became the American states of Florida and Georgia. General James Oglethorpe repulsed a Spanish regiment in the Battle of Bloody Marsh, thereby holding the area for the English.

Lord and Lieutenant
General Cornwallis
Engraver Unknown
(Plate 36032)

George III had the good luck of being King when George Washington led the colonies to Independence. George Washington fought against **Lord Cornwallis** (1738—1805) and accepted Cornwallis's surrender at Yorktown, which was the last major land battle of the American Revolutionary War, and resulted in the capture of 7,000 British soldiers.

George III was the first Hanoverian king to have English as his first language, and to be born in England. He was the longest reigning monarch in British history, and had 15 children. Finally, he succumbed to madness, and died in 1820. He was succeeded by his son, King George IV.

25

The bookplate of **Queen Charlotte Sophia of Mecklenburg** (1744—1818), German born wife of King George III, is shown on the right. They had 15 children, including a son, the Prince of Wales, who became King George IV.

They were the first royalty to live in Buckingham Palace. She was an avid listener of music, and entertained Handel, Bach and Mozart at various times. She was an amature botanist, receiving plantings from explorers Captain James Cook and Sir Joseph Banks which she planted in her gardens at Kew. She also founded orphanages, and provided funds for the General Lying-in Hospital for expectant mothers.

The Queen had a close correspondence with Marie Antoinette of France, and was said to be shocked and overwhelmed at Antoinette's execution. Queen Charlotte died about a year before her husband. Several places are named after her, including Charlotte, North Carolina.

Princess Sophia, Daughter of George III
Engraver Unknown
(Plate 36028)

Princess Sophia (1777—1848) was the 12th child of King George III. He preferred his daughters over his sons and hoped to find suitable husbands for them, but his wife, Charlotte of Mecklenburg-Strelitz, wanted her daughters next to her, chaste and subservient. The daughters referred to their life style in the House of Hanover as living in a nunnery. This strategy didn't work so well with Sophia, who was rumoured to have had a child out of wedlock, either from a love match with one of her father's personal attendants or from being raped by her older brother, the Duke of Cumberland.

At the end of her life, Sophia lived in the home of her neice, Princess Victoria who later became Queen Victoria, at Kensington Palace.

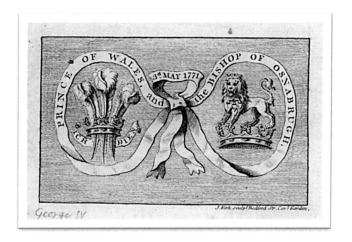

King George IV
Engraver J. Kirk
(Plate 36004)

King George IV (1762—1830) was the son of King George III. Effectively, he was the Prince Regent from 1811 to 1820 during his father's illness, and was the king from 1820 until his own death in 1830. During his reign, George IV saw victory in the Napoleonic wars when Sir Arthur Wellesley defeated Napoleon at Waterloo.

George IV lived a rather profligate life, secretly married a commoner when he was 18, had several mistresses and spent huge amounts of money. He spoke English, French, German and Italian. George Singleton Copley painted a portrait of King George IV. The engraver of King George IV's plate was J. Kirk of Bedford Garden.

Arthur Wellesley
Engraver Unknown
(Plate 36001)

Sir Arthur Wellesley, 1st Duke of Wellington (1769—1852) became Prime Minister in 1828, and granted full civil rights to Catholics, a move decried by the more nationalistic and protestant politicians, resulting in a pistol duel whereby both parties conveniently missed the other.

Wellesley did not do well at Eaton, and thus was educated in Europe. His first love was music, but he ended up with a political and military career, eventually defeating Napoleon. He fought at Flanders, and directed the campaign in India.

Even while in Parliament, he fought military campaigns in Portugal and France. He is regarded as one of the top 100 Britons of all time, and as a military genius whose battle strategies are still studied at military academies.

27

General Henry Wyndham (1790—1860) was a conservative politician and Member of Parliament after finishing his military career. While in the British army Wyndham fought and was badly wounded at the Battle of Waterloo as a Captain and Lieutenant Colonel in charge of the Coldstream Guards. Captain Wyndham was one of three soldiers who closed the gate a Hougoumont, an action that stopped the French from over-running the English troops and became a turning point in the battle which led to the defeat of Napoleon at Waterloo.

King George IV's Prime Minister, **The Honorable Spencer Perceval** (1762—1812), was assassinated while in office. After King George IV, the political rule of England resided primarily with the Prime Minister. Among them was The Right Honorable **Benjamin Disraeli** (Plate 36039) and **William Ewart Gladstone** (Plate 36036, 36037).

Benjamin Disraeli (1804—1881), the only Jewish Prime Minister in England's history, served in that office twice, alternating with William Gladstone who served four times as Prime Minister. While Disraeli was Prime Minister representing the conservative party, Queen Victoria became Empress of India, the Second Anglo-Afghan War was lost, the Zulu War in Africa took place, and he arranged for England to purchase a major interest in the Suez Canal. Among his many accomplishments, Disraeli wrote over a dozen novels including *Vivian Gray*, *The Rise of Iskander*, *Infernal Marriage*, *Henrietta Temple*, and *Lothair*.

Benjamin Disraeli
Engraver Unknown
(Plate 36039)

William Ewart
Gladstone
Prime Minister of England 4 times
Engraver Unknown
(Plate 36036)

William Ewart Gladstone (1809—1898) became England's longest serving Prime Minister although his terms were interrupted by Benjamin Disraeli's conservative victories. Whereas Disraeli became the friend of Queen Victoria, Gladstone was not liked by the Queen. Gladstone introduced the concept of 'secret voting' to the English public and favored Irish independence, but also spoke in favor of the Confederate States of America during the American Civil War.

Early in his political life, Gladstone took on the rescue and rehabilitation of prostitutes, sometimes himself walking the streets of London to talk with and help women of the street. He founded "the Church Penitentiary Association for Fallen Women" and spent a lot of time arranging for employment of women who needed help. Accused of taking advantage of some of these women, Gladstone won a court case which totally exonerated him. The initials of the engraver of Gladstone's plate below are T.E.H.

The bookplate and photographs of Austrian **Archduke Maximilian** (1832—1867) who was installed by Napoleon as the Emperor of Mexico in 1864 contrary to the sense of the Monroe Doctrine which said no foreign incursions should take place in the Western hemisphere. In 1865, the U.S. told the French troops to get out of Mexico. The Emperor was imprisoned, and later executed. **Queen Charlotte of Belgium** (1840—1927), Maximilian's wife, went insane when she could not get help for her husband's release from either Napoleon or the Pope. She died in 1927.

A newspaper clipping said Maximilian paid the price for having been a European emperor on the American continent June 19, 1867. He was executed, carrying a cross, by the order of Benito Juarez, who became president after carrying out the execution. Along with him were ex-President Miramon, who had invited in the French, and General Mejia who opposed Benito Juarez in the revolution.

Newspaper clipping
Photographer Unknown

June 19, 1867 Archduke Maximilian, ex-President Miramon, and General Mejia face a firing squad ordered by Benito Juarez, a Zapotec Indian who led the revolution in Mexico. Maximilian was 35 years old.

Albert, Prince of Wales, husband of Queen Victoria
Engraver Unknown
(Plate 18125)

The **Prince of Wales (Albert)** (1819—1861) was married to Queen Victoria from 1840 to his death in 1861. He became her chief advisor, masterminded the Great Exhibition of 1851 that celebrated the British industrial age, and the expansion of the Empire. Albert may have averted a war with the United States by intervening diplomatically in the Trent Affair.

Queen Victoria reigned 63 years 7 months, the longest of any female monarch up until that time in history. The Queen and Albert had nine children and forty-two grandchildren. The straight-laced British public didn't like Prince Albert because his father divorced his mother because of her adultery, an activity highly prevalent during Victorian times. Most of their children married into the royal families of Europe.

31

George Frederick Ernest Albert, Prince of Wales
King George V
Engraver Unknown
(Plate 36030)

George Frederick Ernest Albert, Prince of Wales and King George V (1865—1936) King of the United Kingdom and the British Dominions and the Emperor of India, was the grandson of Queen Victoria and Prince Albert, and also was the cousin of Tsar Nicholas II of Russia and the cousin of Kaiser Wilhelm II of Germany. His mother was the eldest daughter of King Christian IX of Denmark.

During his reign, King George V saw the rise of socialism, communism, fascism, Irish republicanism, and the Indian Independence movement. He had the misfortune of being at war with the country—Germany--of his cousin during the First World War.

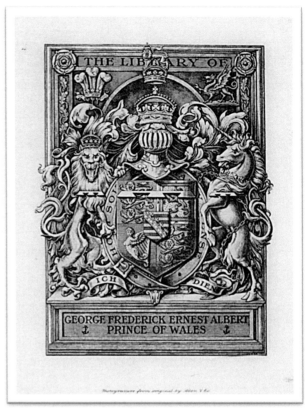

In 1931, the British Empire recognized the separate countries as pieces of the Commonwealth nations that were separate, Independent states.

Sir Thomas North Dick Lauder of Grange
Engraver Charles William Sherborn
(Plate 28003)

The history of the Lauder baronetcy of Fountainhall, Haddingtonshire began in 1625 with Sir John Lauder and continues to this day with Martin Dick Lauder born in 1976. **Sir Thomas North Dick Lauder** was born in 1846 and died in 1919. Each figure and motto in the bookplate is symbolic of one of the baronetcies.

Cyril Flower, later the first Lord Battersea (1843—1907), was a British liberal politician who served in the third Gladstone government. He was married to Constance Rothschild of the English banking family, and was a patron of the arts especially favoring the work of James McNeil Whistler.

32

Lord Battersea
Engraver Charles William Sherborn
(Plate 28009)

John Alexander, Marquis of Bath descends from Sir John Thynne the elder who was born in 1515 and was the builder of Longleat. Longleat is a stately mansion designed in the Elizabethan style, with a maze or hedge sculpted with trails famous for becoming lost in. It was previously an Augustinian priory.

Second Lieutenant John Alexander, Viscount Wymouth's bookplate was engraved by Charles William Sherborn; Alexander was killed in World War I.

John Alexander Marquess of Bath
Engraver Charles William Sherborn
(Plate 28022)

William Lygon, the 7th Earl Beauchamp (1872—1938), was the governor of New South Wales, Australia, but resigned when his homosexuality became known. Although he was succeeded by the 8ᵗʰ Earl Beauchamp, the title became extinct with the death of the 7th Earl. The family line had existed since 1735, and was a title in the peerage since 1815.

Chapter III: British Authors

The Blackburn Collection contains two folios with 140 bookplates of British authors. Among them are philosophers, politicians, ex libris collectors, historians, etc. Bookplates of some of the more recognizable names are exhibited and discussed below.

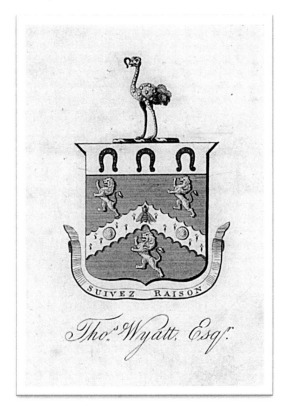

Thomas Wyatt
Engraver Unknown
(Plate 12056)

There were two Thomas Wyatt's, father and son; it is not certain who owned the bookplate—probably both. **Thomas Wyatt the Elder** (1503—1542) was an ambassador to Spain during the time of the Spanish Inquisition, and he was accompanied to Spain by his son **Thomas Wyatt, the Younger** (1521—1554).

The elder Wyatt was a member of Henry VII's Privy Council, and was a counselor to Henry VIII. While serving Henry VIII, Wyatt helped petition for the annulment of the marriage between Henry VIII and Catherine of Argonne so that Henry could marry Anne Boleyn. Anne Boleyn became Henry VIII's 2nd wife. That marriage ended badly, too, with Anne's head in a basket so that Henry could marry Anne Seymour. Anne Boleyn had a daughter, Elizabeth, who became Queen Elizabeth I of England. Some historians believe Wyatt may have seen Boleyn's head fall as he was in prison at the time awaiting his own fate. Fortunately for him, he survived to become High Sherriff of Kent.

Thomas Wyatt the Elder is known for his introduction of the Petrarchan (Italian) sonnet to English literature. He translated several sonnets from the Italian, and wrote several more in English. Petrarch's sonnet structure was characterized by the rhyme scheme abba, abba, cd, cd, cd. The English sonnet structure, later to be known as the Elizabethan or Shakespearean sonnet, followed the rhyming scheme of abab, cdcd, efef, gg and is usually written in iambic pentameter—that is, light accent followed by a heavy accent five times in a line of poetry.

According to his in Wikipedia biographers, Wyatt was "one of the originators of the convention in love poetry according to which the mistress is characterized as hard-hearted and cruel." Several of Shakespeare's sonnets use this characterization of women, as in sonnet 130: "My mistresses' eyes be nothing like the sun…And yet, by heaven, I think my love as rare/ As any she belied with false compare."

Thomas Wyatt the Younger assisted Queen Mary against the rebellion of the Duke of Northumberland, but later because of her intended marriage to Philip of Spain opposed her. Wyatt was caught and beheaded, but not before he managed to sire ten children.

David Hume (1711—1776) is remembered as an early proponent of the philosophy of empiricism and skepticism. In its rudimentary sense, empiricism is the idea that all knowledge is derived from sensory experience, and skepticism is a disbelief in philosophical solutions and a rejection of the external world. One of Hume's arguments was against the notion of proving a linkage between cause and effect.

Thomas Campbell (1777—1844) was a Scottish poet who also produced patriotic war songs including "The Soldier's Dream" and "The Battle of Maqd and Strange Turkish Princes."

Although Campbell remained in England, his father and brothers were tobacco traders; unfortunately, they lost their fortunes because of the American Revolutionary War. After the war, the brothers remained in Virginia, and one married a daughter of Patrick Henry. Campbell played a large part in the planning and founding of the University of London.

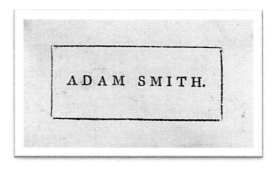

Adam Smith (1723—1790), a Scottish political and moral philosopher wrote *An Enquiry into the Nature and Causes of the Wealth of Nations* which expounds classical free market economic theory that is largely the basis for conservative economists worldwide even today. Prime Minister Margaret Thatcher was said to carry a copy of the *Wealth of Nations* in her handbag.

John Hall Stevenson
Engraver Unknown
(Plate 25029)

John Hall, later **John Hall Stevenson** (1718—1789) after taking the last name of his wife, was memorialized as Eugenius in his friend Lawrence Sterne's novel, *Tristram Shandy*. Stevenson grew up in Skelton Castle which he later inherited and turned into a site dubbed Crazy Castle for his club of demoniacs that had as its principle activity drinking and orgies. As a writer, Stevenson's fame came from writing licentious poetry including "Lyric Epistle", "Fables for Grown Gentlemen", and "Crazy Tales". He claimed to be a friend of Horace Walpole and Rousseau.

William Cowper
Engraver Unknown
(Plate 33047)

William Cowper (1731—1800) was an early humorist and poet who wrote of everyday life and is credited as being a precursor of romantic poetry. He was admired by William Wordsworth and Samuel Taylor Coleridge, and was a friend of John Newton who wrote "Amazing Grace."

William Cowper translated the *Iliad* and the *Odyssey* of Homer into blank verse. Unfortunately, he also dreamed that he was doomed to eternal damnation and tried three times to commit suicide.

Edward Gibbon
Engraver Unknown
(Plate 25018)

The Decline and Fall of the Roman Empire was written by **Edward Gibbon** (1737—1794) over a period of several years, the first volume of six being publish in 1776. Later volumes were banned in several countries because of Gibbon's 'scathing critique of Christianity'. Winston Churchill, however, said he was highly influenced by the *Decline and Fall* and Gibbon's work was well regarded by other contemporaries and successors in the literary world.

Gibbon never married; he proposed to a Swiss woman named Suzanne Churchod but both of their fathers objected. She later married a French aristocrat and became the mother of the French writer, Madame de Stael.

Anna Damer
Engraver Unknown
(Plate 23016)

Anna Seymour Damer (1749—1828) was a sculptress who worked in the neoclassical style producing sculptures in bronze, terracotta, and marble. She traveled and studied in Europe, visited France and secured an audience with Napoleon. She was known as a patron of all the arts, and developed friendships with writers, actors, playwrights, artists and musicians. She was reputed to have had a lesbian relationship with the author Mary Berry.

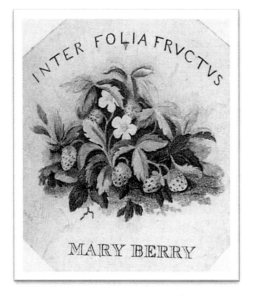

Mary Berry
Engraver Unknown
(Plate 23008)

Mary Berry (1763—1852) and her sister Agnes were closely acquainted with Horace Walpole who wrote a novel called *The Castle of Otranto*. Walpole was the son of the first Prime Minister of England. At age 70, Walpole became enamored with the Berry sisters, and referred to them as his twin wives, once signing his name as 'Fondleberry'. Walpole didn't marry either sister, but left each of them a sizable fortune and his estate Strawberry Hill when he died. The Berry sisters were together all of their lives into their nineties.

Thomas Pennant (1726—1798) was a Welsh naturalist who wrote several books including *British Zoology, History of Quadrupeds, Artic Zoology,* and *Indian Zoology*. He also collected books, mainly of scientific interest, that are now in the National Library of Wales.

W. H. Ireland
Engraver Unknown
(Plate 26038)

William Henry Ireland (1777—1835) earned fame as a forger of fictitious Shakespearean documents. Since there were no known actual written documents in the hand of William Shakespeare other than his plays, Ireland created some, as well as two new plays, *Vortigem and Rowena*, and *Henry II*. Apparently the forgeries were good enough that Boswell and the sitting poet laureate of England, Henry James Pye, proclaimed them to be authentic. Unfortunately everybody's reputation, especially Ireland's (and his father's, who participated in the hoax) was ridiculed. Although the *Vortigem* play was performed in 1796, it didn't again appear on a stage again until 2008. W.H. Ireland died in poverty.

Newstead Abby, Home of Lord Byron
Engraver Unknown
(Plate 25020)

Every student of English literature and history has heard of **George Gordon, Lord Byron** (1788—1824), John Keats, and Percy Bysshe Shelly, whose poetry written over a very few years of their short lives is as readable today as it was then. Byron is known for writing *Childe Harold's Pilgrimage*, *Don Juan*, and "She Walks in Beauty".

He was the most flamboyant of the Romantic writers, famous for incurring huge debts, having numerous love affairs with members of both sexes, and may have incestuously slept with his half-sister. Byron died after joining the fight for Greek independence from the Turkish Ottoman Empire which lasted until another Englishman, T. E. Lawrence (of Arabia), helped organize the Arab Revolt early in the 20th century. Byron is regarded as a hero to the Greeks.

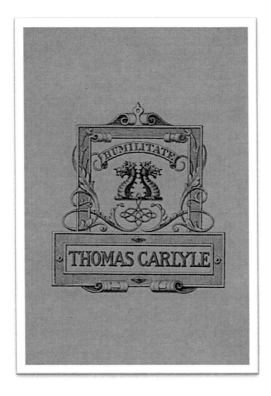

Thomas Carlyle
Engraver Unknown
(Plate 26010)

A Scottish philosopher, satirical writer, essayist, historian, and teacher, **Thomas Carlyle** (1795—1881) called economics "the dismal science." He came from a family of strict Calvinists, but lost his faith in Christianity while attending the University of Edinburgh. Carlyle wrote a number of books, one being *The French Revolution: A History* (1837) that was used by Charles Dickens for source material when writing *A Tale of Two Cities*. Many of Carlyle's works can be obtained through Project Gutenberg.

The engraver of Thomas Carlyle's bookplate is unknown, but Oscar Taylor Blackburn created a bookplate for a member of a later generation, Alonzo F. Carlyle, using a similar design. A painting of Thomas Carlyle was done by James McNeill Whistler in 1872.

Thomas Hood
Engraver Unknown
(Plate 33042)

Thomas Hood (1799—1845) was a poet, engraver and father of a successful playwright with the same name. Hood was famous for his humorous poetry, and puns.
He wrote:

"However critics may take offence,
A double meaning has double sense."

40

One of the most prolific writers in English history, **Anthony Trollope** (1815—1882) wrote forty-seven novels, including two six volume sets called the *Chronicles of Barsetshire* and the Palliser Novels, respectively. He also wrote a dozen short stories, eighteen works of nonfiction, and two plays. His mother made a living from writing; Anthony Trollope worked for the postal department and did much of his writing while traveling.

Anthony Trollope
Engraver Unknown
(Plate 25023)

Sir Richard
Burton
Engraver Unknown
(Plate 26014

Sir Richard Burton (1821—1890) was truly a 'renaissance man' who lived a most amazing life. His Wikipedia biographers write that he was 'a geographer, soldier, explorer, translator, writer, orientalist, cartographer, ethnologist, spy, linguist, poet, Egyptologist, fencer and diplomat.'

Burton served in the British military in India, where he learned Persian, Urdu, Hindu, and several other Indian dialects. During his life, he mastered over 50 languages and dialects, wrote books that are still used in India as school text books, translated the *Kama Sutra* and *The Thousand and One Nights* (classics that are still in print), and worked on a book called *The Perfumed Garden* by Sheikh Nafwazi reputed to be an Arabic work with erotic themes like the *Kama Sutra*.

Burton also wrote several ethnographic works including one about his journey to Mecca disguised as an Afghan at a time which if discovered he would have been killed. His identity was nearly was uncovered when seen urinating in the desert standing up in the European manner; Burton is rumored to have killed his discoverer to maintain his disguise. This was probably just a rumor, possibly started by Burton himself. Biographies of his life read like novels.

Burton was an ambassador in Africa, a traveler to the United States and South America, and one of the explorers engaged in the discovery of the source of the Nile River.

He married somewhat late in life, but had no children due to a venereal infection that he may have given to his wife. There are stories about how upon his death she destroyed all of his unfinished literary works including his draft of *The Perfumed Garden*, but she denied burning anything of literary value.

Although Burton was probably the most prolific and knowledgeable writer of his generation, British academic circles did not hold him in high regard during his lifetime.

George Meredith
Engraver Unknown
(Plate 26017)

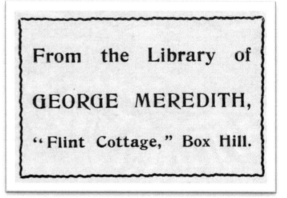

George Meredith (1828—1909) was an English novelist and poet. Among his books was *The Ordeal of Richard Feverel* (1859) which has been called the first modern novel in English literature. It is a psychological exploration of the inability of education to control the passions, and examines the restrictive sexual morality of Meredith's day. Another novel, *The Egoist*, was about the subjugation of women in Victorian life. He has 14 books of poetry and 19 novels to his credit. Although not considered a major English writer today, George Meredith wrote 19 novels including *The Case of General Opal and Lady Camper* (1877), and the two poems "Lark Ascending" and "Lucifer in Starlight".

Arthur Conan Doyle had Sherlock Holmes say "Let's talk of George Meredith...we shall leave minor lesser matters until tomorrow" and Oscar Wilde said of Meredith "...his style is chaos illumined by flashes of lightening." Among Meredith's friends were Dante Gabriel Rossetti, Algernon Charles Swinburne, Robert Louis Stevenson and J. M. Barrie.

Algernon Charles Swinburne
Engraver Unknown
(Plate 33040)

Algernon Charles Swinburne (1837—1909) was an English poet, playwright, novelist and literary critic who was nominated eight times for a Nobel Prize in literature (but not selected). Swinburne wrote nine verse plays, sixteen volumes of poetry, and literary criticism about William Blake, the Bronte' sisters, Victor Hugo, Ben Johnson and several works about William Shakespeare. He was reputed to be a 'decadent' poet but Oscar Wilde---no stranger to poetic decadence himself—said Swinburne was "...a braggart in matters of vice, who had done everything he could do to convince his fellow citizens of his homosexuality and bestiality without being to the slightest degree a homosexual or beastilizer."

Joseph B. Priestly
Engraver Unknown
(Plate 26035)

Joseph B. Priestly (1894—1984), a contemporary of Winston Churchill, was almost as famous. He wrote a novel, *The Good Companions*, and several plays including *An Inspector Calls*, and *Dragon's Mouth*. He was a broadcaster with the BBC, and all together wrote 26 novels, 13 plays and several other works of literary criticism, social and political treatises.

Thomas Burke (1886—1945) was known as the laureate of London's Chinatown because of his portrayals of street life by using a Chinese character to tell his stories. Besides novels, he wrote the short stories "Limehouse Nights" "The Sun in Splendor"

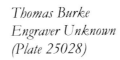

Thomas Burke
Engraver Unknown
(Plate 25028)

and "The Wind and the Rain: a book of confessions" As reflected in the art deco style of his bookplate, much of Burke's writing was done and set in the 1920s.

43

Margot Tennant, Lady Asquith
Engraver Unknown
(Plate 23005)

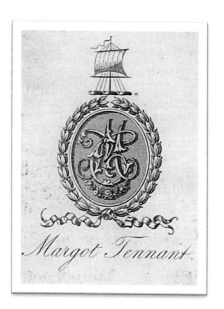

Margot Tennant (1862—1945) married Herbert Henry Asquith who became a liberal Prime Minister of England during the First World War. Margot was an outspoken socialite who expressed some sentiments in favor of the Germans which didn't earn her a lot of love in England.

Alfred, Lord Tennyson Engraver Unknown (Plate 33018)

Several of **Alfred, Lord Tennyson's** (1809—1892) bookplates were signed, as is the one from the Blackburn Collection. He was the poet laureate of Great Britain and Ireland for much of Queen Victoria's reign, and wrote the phrases "Tis better to have loved and lost/than never to have loved at all" and "Theirs is not to reason why/theirs is but to do and die."

Most students have read "Grey's Elegy," "The Charge of the Light Brigade", and "Crossing the Bar" by Tennyson. He is the ninth most quoted writer according to the *Oxford Dictionary of Quotations*.

Five novels of **Thomas Hardy** (1840—1948), *Far From the Madding Crowd* (1874), *The Mayor of Castorbridge* (1886), *Tess of the d'Urbervilles* (1891), *The Return of the Native* (1878), and *Jude the Obscure* (1895) are recognized as classics and have been reprinted several times over. Hardy wrote poetry and several dozen short stories. He is known as a Victorian realist because his writing is often critical of Victorian society. Among the persons who Hardy was influenced by were John Stuart Mill and his philosophy of utilitarianism and August Comte, a founder of sociology and philosophy of positivism.

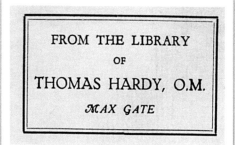

Thomas Hardy
Engraver Unknown
(Plate 26047)

44

"The Great Game" a phrase coined by **Rudyard Kipling** (1865—1936) in his novel of British spies in India, *Kim*, was prescient of the global machinations taking place in the late 20th and early 21st centuries. The modern great game is being played out against a backdrop of American, Russian, Chinese, Indian, Pakistani, Afghan and Iranian political and military maneuvering, much the same as it was during the 19th and early 20th centuries.

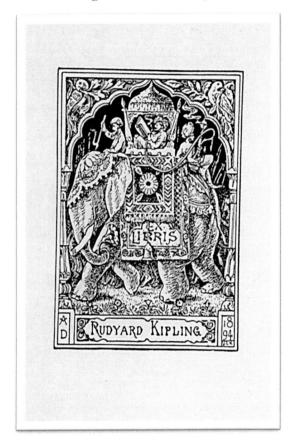

Rudyard Kipling
Engraver Unknown
(Plate 26056)

No longer a battle primarily for strategic positioning, the wars in Afghanistan and now the former Russian satellite countries are being fought as proxies for the cold war between the US and Russia, not much different from those anticipated by Kipling. Kipling saw the Great Game as a struggle of foreign nations for strategic and territorial control of Afghanistan then including Pakistan to act as a buffer against Russian incursions into India.

Rudyard Kipling was the first English language recipient of the Nobel Prize for Literature in 1907. He wrote novels, short stories, poetry and nonfiction that are still being read today and are the subject of movies and documentaries. Among the most famous are the novels *Kim* and *The Jungle Book*. Kipling's short stories include "Riki Tiki Tavi", "The Man Who Would Be King" and "The Phantom Rickshaw". Two of his most famous poems are "The Road to Mandalay" and "Gunga Din".

Much of Kipling's writing portrays the experience of British soldiers in India during the late Victorian period. He was born in India, educated in England, returned to India in later life, and traveled throughout the world including the United States. His writing was looked down upon during the 20th century as being thought too shallow, but with the wars in Afghanistan and the ongoing struggle for Central Asia by the Western powers, he is more widely read and appreciated today.

William Butler Yeats
Engraver T. Sturge Moore
(Plate 25058)

The most important Irish poet of the 20th century, **William Butler Yeats** (1865—1939) was the driving force behind the Irish Literary Revival. He, and several others including his friend and engraver T. Sturge Moore who also signed the bookplate, were instrumental in starting the Irish Literary Theatre and the Abby Theatre in Dublin which wished to express the 'ascendency of the playwright rather than the actor-manager a l'anglais. W. B. Yeats participated in most aspects of the theatre, especially through writing and revival of Irish plays.

W. B. Yeats was born in Dublin into an artistic family. His father studied art, and his brother Jack, whose bookplate is shown below, became a highly esteemed painter.

Early in life, Yeats fell in love with an Irish nationalist named Maud Goone. He proposed to her three times over the years but was refused. Aften an unsuccessful marriage, she later spent time with Yeats, their relationship finally resulting in a one night only consumation. Of this night, Yeats wrote "the tragedy of sexual intercourse is the perpetual virginity of the soul." He later married a younger woman, Bertha Georgie Hyde Lees, with whom he had two children.

It would be difficult to name the best of Yeats work since it is all good. During his lifetime and after he enjoyed world-wide recognition and was awarded the Nobel Prize for Literature in 1923. He served in the first Irish senate, and was an advocate for nationalism over partition of Ireland from England. His contemporary and poet W.H. Auden, wrote in memory of Yeats,

"Earth, receive and honored guest;
William Yeats is laid to rest.
Let the Irish vessel lie
Emptied of its poetry. …"

George aka Georgie Yeats
Engraver Thomas Sturge Moore
(Plate 22002)

Bertha Georgie Hyde Lees Yeats (1892—1968) became the wife of William Butler Yeats in 1917. She was about 25, he was 51. At the time, she was immersed in London's avant-guarde social circles; her best friend was married to the poet Ezra Pound, and her best friend's mother was once the lover of her future husband, William Butler Yeats. Nevertheless, they married and had two children. Their's was a distant and remote relationship; he was possessed by his poetry, and she raised their family and attended to her husband and his literary legacy. Yeats became part of the Irish nationalist movement; consequently, their existence was threatened, once having a tower blown up outside their door. For his wife, Yeats wrote a short poem called "To be carved on a stone at Thoor Ballylee":

> "I, the poet William Yeats,
> With old mill-boards and sea green slates
> And smithy work from Gort forge
> Restored this tower for my wife George".

Jack Yeats
Engraver Jack B. Yeats
(Plate 30036)

Jack B. Yeats (1871—1957) was William Butler Yeats' brother. He was the son of a portrait artist, and has been acclaimed as Ireland's most important artist in the 20th century. His early paintings were landscapes, but later he moved on to other subjects. After being identified as belonging to the Romantic Movement in art, Yeats became an Expressionist with elements of modernism in his work.

In addition to painting, Jack B. Yeats was a writer. Once he wrote a parody of Sherlock Holmes that he called "Chubb Lock Homes" for a comic publication. He worked in the Irish theatre, designing sets, writing and staging plays, and was a close friend of Thomas Beckett. He wrote novels, using a stream-of-consciousness style of writing that characterized James Joyce's writing. Besides being a painter whose paintings now sell for over $1 million, novelist, and playwright, Jack Yeats has the distinction of being Ireland's first Olympic medalist, an award he received for an artistic entry.

Charles Dickens
Commemorative Stamp
Engraver Unknown
(Plate 38023)

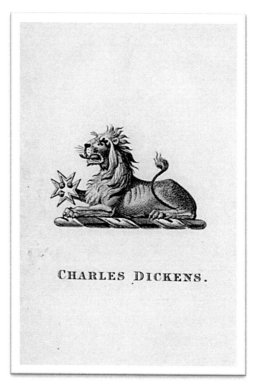

Charles Dickens
Engraver Unknown
(Plate 38022)

Except for William Shakespeare, **Charles Dickens** (1812—1912) is the most recognized writer in British history. During his lifetime, he and his books achieved an unbelievable amount of fame. Dickens' appearances doing readings from his books always resulted in packed houses. Most of his books are still in print, and some of them, such as *A Christmas Carol* and *A Tale of Two Cities*, are regularly made into movies or television dramas. Like many others, Oscar Taylor Blackburn was a fan of Charles Dickens, collected much of his memorabilia, and through his antiquarian bookstore sold many first editions of Charles Dickens' work.

Wilke Collins (1824—1889), a friend of Charles Dickens, wrote two novels himself, The Lady in White, and The Moonstone. Collins' novels are mysteries, and he is credited with being one of the earliest writers using that genre. His novels are considered classics and are still in print.

The letter reproduced below was written by Wilke Collins in 1878, and was among the items found in the Dickens folio in the Blackburn Collection.

Charles Kingsley (1819—1875) was first a priest, then a professor, historian, and novelist. He corresponded with Charles Darwin, became a Chaplin to Queen Victoria, and was the private tutor to the Prince of Wales, the future King Edward VII. Kingsley wrote several scientific papers, and some of his novels were concerned with unsanitary conditions found in British cities. He also wrote children's books, and novels with a political message.

Kingsley was a member of the 1866 Edward Eyre Defense Committee that defended Eyre's suppression of an uprising known as the Morant Bay Rebellion that resulted in the deaths of dozens of rebelling Jamaicans because of orders given by Governor Eyre. Eyre was charged and exonerated, but because the punishments for the rebellion were so brutal, including executions, imprisonments, floggings and home burnings, the matter is still controversial. It was a turning point in Jamaican history and independence.

Charles Kingsley
Engraver Unknown
(Plate 25017)

Justin McCarthy
Engraver Unknown
(Plate 25008)

Justin McCarthy (1830—1912) began writing at a young age. He was a journalist, historian, and Irish nationalist, member of the Parliament of Great Britain, politician, and novelist. He wrote a history of the Victorian period called the *History of Our Time*, and a *History of the Four Georges*. He wrote several novels, four of them titled *A Fair Saxon, Dear Lady Disdain, Miss Misanthrope* and *Donna Quixote*. Some of his books are available through the Gutenberg Project.

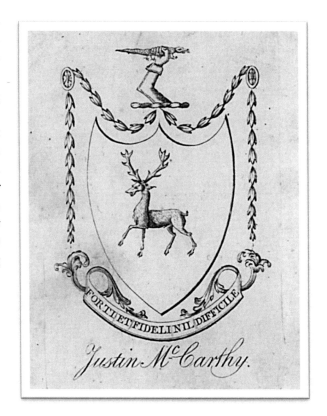

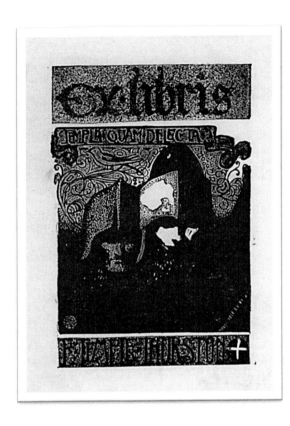

Ernest Temple (Thurston) (1879—1933) wrote 40 books, 17 of which became the basis for movies. He also wrote plays including The Wandering Jew and a novel called *The City of Beautiful Nonsense* (1909). His bookplate is very rare.

The English writer, **Enoch Arnold Bennett** (1867—1931), grew up in Hanley, the Potteries of Staffordshire, England which became the site of several of his fictional works. In 1903, he moved to France, married, and wrote several novels. He said he was inspired by de Maupassant.

His most famous works—he wrote 40 novels and books of short stories—are *The Old Wives' Tale* and *Anna of Five Towns*, the latter made into a television series.

Besides fiction, Bennett wrote 16 books of non-fiction, the script for one film, and an opera titled *Don Juan de Manera*. A French omlette, Omlette Arnold Bennett, is named after him because he liked it so much and ordered it every time he went to a restaurant.

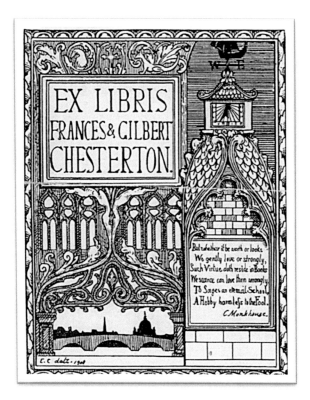

G. K. Chesterton
Engraver E. C.
(Plate 25007)

Gilbert Keith Chesterton (1874—1936) was a philosopher, dramatist, journalist, orator, literary and art critic, biographer, and novelist. He created the fictional priest-detective Father Brown that has been a featured series in public television's Masterpiece Theater. Chesterton wrote about 80 books, 200 short stories, 4,000 essays and several plays.

Chapter IV: American Presidents, Politicians and Warriors

William Penn
Engraver Unknown
(Plate 27005)

Although the story of the settlement of America by the English begins several decades earlier, the earliest American bookplate found in the Blackburn collection dated 1703 is that of **William Penn** (1644—1718), the English founder of the Province of Pennsylvania.

Penn's father was owed a substantial amount of money by the reigning King Charles II of England, who after Penn's father's death awarded William Penn a large tract of land in the New World in lieu of payment of the debt. Penn went there, established a colony which he named Pennsylvania and became its Proprietor.

William Penn was a friend of George Fox, the founder of the Quakers who vowed to bow to no man. Early in life, Penn was subject to several court cases in which he was imprisoned. When he designed his new settlement in the New World, Penn drafted a 'Charter of Liberties' that included the guarantee of a free and fair trial by jury, freedom of religion, freedom from unjust imprisonment, and free elections. The colony of Pennsylvania became a favored destination for other persecuted religionists from Europe.

Quakers, Huguenots, Mennonites, Amish and Lutherans came to Pennsylvania. Philadelphia, designed by Penn, is still known as the city of brotherly love. Even in his dealings with American Indians, Penn was (and still is) known for his fairness. Juries in matters about offenses against Indians were to be made up of half Indians and half immigrants. Penn died penniless in England having been swindled out of his fortune, but his American reputation is intact.

William Byrd II of Westover (1674—1744) was the second in a line of Byrd's in Virginia, his father being the first. The elder Byrd was an Indian trader and importer of slaves, and established the beginnings of a family dynasty that continues to this day although the Westover plantation was sold out of the Byrd family in 1814.

William Byrd was born in Virginia and raised on the James River plantation, but spent most of his youth in England, where he was educated, eventually matriculating from the Middle Temple in London with a law degree. Byrd was a colonial representative in England, and while there became a member of the Royal Society.

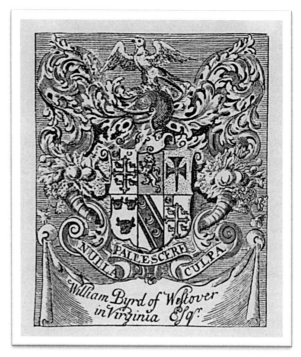

William Byrd returned to England in 1705 to manage a plantation that eventually grew to 179,000 acres. He was a staunch supporter of the plantation system, and represented owners whenever necessary. Byrd married, had four daughters and a son, and amassed the largest library in Virginia at the time of 4,000 volumes.

One of William Byrd II of Westover's accomplishments was to write diaries that provided a historical characterization of the economic life of large plantations. Among the titles were *A Journey to the Land of Eden, A Progress to the Mines*, and *The Secret Diary of William Byrd of Westover 1709—1712*. One of the *Secret Diary* entries reads, "In the evening my wife and little Jenny (a slave) had a great quarrel in which my wife got the worst but at last by the help of the family Jenny was overcome and soundly whipped. At night I ate some bread and cheese. …"

George Washington
Engraver Unknown
(Plate 20001)

George Washington (1732—1799) became the Chief of the Continental Army after serving as a senior officer in the French and Indian War. At the behest of Alexander Hamilton and again by the Continental Congress, Washington became the Senior Officer of the Army which went on to defeat the British armies led by General Cornwallis (Plate 36032).

Washington presided over the convention that drafted the Constitution of the United States, and was the first United States President.

George Washington
Photographer Unknown
(Plate 20002)

Henry Dawkins
Engraver Henry Dawkins
(Plate 20040)

An interesting historical note is that **Henry Dawkins** (1753—1786), a silversmith and engraver of bookplates, together with a fellow would-be counterfeiter named Isaac Ketcham were thrown in prison after their counterfeiting plan was exposed. Dawkins may have had too much alcohol for his own good.

Ketcham's paper supplier reported the suspected counterfeiters to the authorities. In jail, they overheard a plot to capture George Washington which, when exposed, helped to secure their own release. Besides bookplates, Dawkins did several other engravings of historical value.

Bushrod Washington
Engraver Unknown
(Plate 20037)

Bushrod Washington (1762—1829) was a nephew of the President and inherited Mt. Vernon after George Washington died. Bushrod was appointed to the Supreme Court by then President John Adams and voted with Federalist and Chief justice John Marshall most of them time. Like his more famous uncle, Bushrod Washington owned and sold slaves during his lifetime.

Paul Revere
Engraver Paul Revere
(Plate 20034)

Paul Revere (1735—1818) was also an engraver and silversmith and may have engraved one of Washington's bookplates, but is better known to schoolchildren because of a line in Longfellow's poem "Listen my children and you shall hear/Of the midnight ride of Paul Revere…"

Besides his own, Paul Revere engraved only six or seven bookplates, which Blackburn's notes indicate are exceedingly rare. There are a very few known copies of Paul Revere's bookplate. The names on the bookplates that Paul Revere signed include Gardiner Chandler, Epes Sargent, William Wetmore, David Greene, Andrew Oliver, Isaiah Thomas, and Pereze Morton. The Gardiner Chandler plate is shown below.

Gardiner Chandler
Engraver Paul Revere
(Restrike Plate 30059)

A 'restrike' plate means that the original plate was cleaned and a new set of prints made from it, likely in Paul Revere's case not by his hand. The design was the same as Revere used in a silver engraving for Lucretia Chandler.

The **Charles E. Goodspeed** bookplate has Paul Revere's Boston Massacre also known as the Bloody Massacre in King Street, Boston 1770 as the pictorial inset with the border engraved by **Sydney L. Smith** (1845—1929).

John Adams (1735—1826) was the second President of the United States and the father of the sixth president. Before becoming president, John Adams had appointed George Washington as head of the Continental army, and served with Washington as the first vice president.

Adams' influence in the development of American political and governmental philosophy is immense, and after his own presidency he wrote the constitution for the state of Massachusetts, and assisted Thomas Jefferson in writing the Declaration of Independence. John Adams was the first President to reside in the White House. Adams was an opponent of slavery, and never bought nor owned a slave. His wife, Abagail Adams, the mother of John Quincy Adams, was a frequent correspondent with her husband which accounts for much of his written legacy.

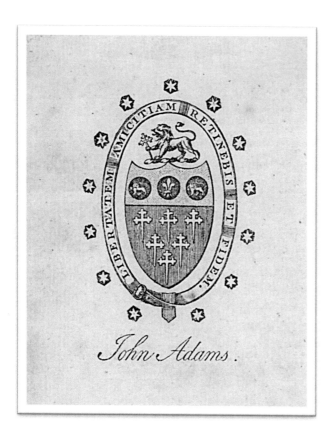

John Adams
Engraver Unknown
(Plate 20028)

Thomas Jefferson
Photographer Unknown
(Plate 20009)

Thomas Jefferson (1743-1826) became the third President of the United States after having served as John Adam's Vice President. During his political career, Jefferson was Governor of Virginia, U.S. Minister to France, a delegate to the Congress of Confederation, and a delegate to the 2nd Continental Congress. Aaron Burr, who killed Alexander Hamilton in a duel, was Jefferson's Vice President. While president, Jefferson obtained $2,500 from Congress to secretly fund the Lewis and Clark Expedition, which led to the Louisiana Purchase in 1803.

Following his presidency, Thomas Jefferson founded, designed and built the University of Virginia, and his home at Monticello where he is now buried. During his lifetime, Jefferson owned as many as 600 slaves whom he used on his 5,000 acre plantation at Monticello. He is said to have fathered several children by one of them, Sally Heming, a contention recently bolstered by DNA evidence.

Marquis de La Fayette (1757—1834), whose full name was Marie-Joseph Paul Yves Roch Gilbert du Motier de La Fayette, became through inheritance a very rich French aristocrat at the age of 12 when his military father was killed by a cannon ball. Impressed by the principles of the American Revolution, La Fayette wrote the French "Declaration of the Rights of Man" having Thomas Jefferson as a consultant. The "Rights of Man" espoused John Locke's natural rights and became a seminal document underlying the French Revolution.

La Fayette was a leader of the French Guarde Nationale. He also served as a general in the American Revolution after leaving France in 1777 disguised as a woman. Besides Washington and Jefferson, La Fayette counted Benjamin Franklin among his friends, and was instrumental in obtaining financial and military support for the Revolution from King Louis XVI.

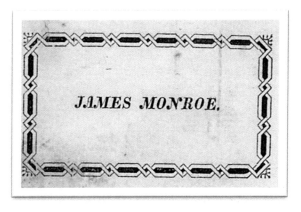

The fifth President of the United States was **James Monroe** (1758—1831). Monroe was the last person to be President who was among the Founding Fathers. He fought in the Revolutionary War, studied law under Thomas Jefferson, and was a delegate in the Continental Congress. Monroe was a senator, Governor of Virginia. Under James Madison, Monroe was Secretary of State and Secretary of War during the War of 1812, and helped negotiate the Louisiana Purchase of 1803. While President, Monroe bought Florida from the Spanish. During his lifetime, James Monroe owned dozens of slaves, and brought some of them with him to the White House.

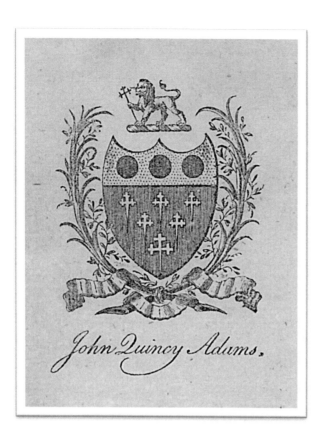

John Quincy Adams
Engraver Unknown
(Plate 20023)

It is not surprising that the Blackburn Collection should have multiple bookplates for **John Quincy Adams** (1767—1848). Adams, who served the United States as diplomat, senator, President, and in the House of Representatives following his presidency, wrote 50 volumes of his diary which historians find the most informative source of information for the period.

John Quincy Adams
Engraver Unknown
(Plate 20024)

At various times, John Quincy Adams was a member of the Federalist, Democratic—Republican, Anti-Masonic and Whig parties. As Secretary of State, Adams negotiated the Treaty of Ghent that ended the War of 1812, obtained Florida from the Spanish, and drafted the Monroe Doctrine. During his service, he directed the United States to pay off its national debt, and later in life initiated the founding of the Smithsonian Institute. Like his father, John Adams, he had a visceral revulsion of slavery and worked to end it.

Philip Schuyler
Engraver Unknown
(Plate 40009)

Philip John Schuyler (1733—1804) was a Revolutionary War general. He had served with the British forces in the French and Indian War, was elected to the Continental Congress of 1775, became Major General of the Continental Army and planned the invasion of Canada. He also was a senator from New York in the first Congress of the United States.

Philip Schuyler married and became the father of 15 children, one of whom married Alexander Hamilton. A statue of Schuyler can be found outside the city hall in Albany, New York.

Alexander Hamilton
Engraver Unknown
(Plate 20036)

Although never president, **Alexander Hamilton** (1755—1804) served in the administrations of Washington and Adams. Hamilton was one of the Founding Fathers of the United States, and became the first Secretary of the Treasury under George Washington, where he created the nations' first financial system. Alexander Hamilton also founded the first political party, and when Washington became president succeeded him as the Senior Officer of the Army. During the Revolutionary War, Hamilton fought in eight major battles.

Hamilton has among his credits the first sex scandal in American governmental history. Hamilton resigned his office when a three year affair with Maria Reynolds became public, and it became known he was paying her husband blackmail money to keep silent. James Monroe and Thomas Jefferson, not the best of friends of Hamilton, exposed the affair.

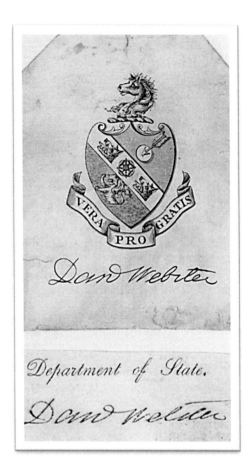

Daniel Webster
Engraver Unknown
(Plate 27003)

Possibly the most eloquent orator ever to inhabit the United States Senate, **Daniel Webster** (1782—1852) was also one of the most controversial. During his 40 years in national public office, he favored slavery and supported "The Compromise of 1850" which included the Fugitive Slave Law of 1850 that legalized the return of runaway slaves. Webster argued for a strong national government, but believed the North and South might separate over the slavery issue, resulting in constant uprisings of black people in the South. Webster resigned from the Senate under a cloud of collegial disdain, but he was appointed Secretary of State under three presidents, Fillmore, Harrison and Tyler. He also unsuccessfully ran for the presidency himself, three times.

Abraham Lincoln
Photographer Unknown
(Plate 20013)

Abraham Lincoln (1809—1865) was born in Hardin County, Kentucky where he lived until he was six years of age. His family moved to Indiana and Illinois. He married Mary Todd in 1842 and they had three children. Mary Todd was from a wealthy family in Lexington, Kentucky, and was once courted by Lincoln's later debating opponent, Stephen Douglas. Although Kentucky was a 'slave state', it chose to stay in the Union during the Civil War.

Lincoln became President of the United States in 1861, just in time to preside over the bloodiest war in American history. The Civil War (1861—1865) ended shortly before Lincoln's assassination in 1865 by John Wilkes Booth at Ford's Theatre in Washington, D.C. Lincoln rose to fame as a Republican through his participation in the Lincoln/Douglas

debates over the slavery issue. While the 16th President of the United States, Lincoln signed the Emancipation Proclamation of 1863 which freed the slaves. After his assassination, his wife said, "The last day he lived was the happiest day of his life."

Mary Todd Lincoln
Photographer Unknown
(Plate 20014)

Mary Todd Lincoln (1818—1882) survived her husband and lived through Reconstruction that is said to have ended in 1777. Before meeting Abraham, Mary Todd had been courted by Steven A. Douglass of the famous Lincoln-Douglass debates. She was a First Lady in the White House, and witness to her husband's murder. She unfortunately suffered from migraine headaches most of her adult life.

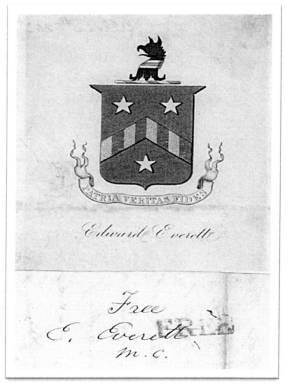

Edward Everett
Engraver Unknown
(Plate 24041)

Edward Everett (1794—1865) preceded Abraham Lincoln in delivering the Gettysburg Address. Everett's address lasted two hours. During his long career, Edward Everett was a United States Congressman, Senator, United States Secretary of State, Governor of Massachusetts, and President of Harvard University. Following their addresses at Gettysburg, Everett sent a message to Lincoln—"I should be glad, if I could flatter myself that I came as near the central idea of the occasion in two hours as you did in two minutes."

SHERMAN

William Tecumseh Sherman (1820—1891) told a secessionist friend before the start of the Civil War, "You people don't know what you are doing. This country will be drenched in blood, and God only knows how it will end. It is all folly, madness, a crime against civilization! … War is a terrible thing."

Sherman served under Ulysses S. Grant, using a 'scorched earth' policy against the Confederate South. He captured Atlanta after the famous 20 mile wide march across Georgia in which he destroyed everything in his path. Later, he accepted the surrender of all Confederate armies of the Carolinas, Georgia, and Florida. Sherman succeeded Grant as the Commanding General of the Army, spent the next fifteen years fighting Indians, and wrote a seminal book on the Civil War.

Harriet Beecher Stowe (1811—1896) came from a family of 13 children; most of her brothers and sisters were social activists during their lives, including several ministers, an early advocate for women's rights, and an influential brother, Henry Ward Beecher. She published one of the most famous novels in American history, *Uncle Tom's Cabin,* in 1851 which became a national best seller. Upon meeting Lincoln, he is credited as saying to Harriet, "So you are the little woman who wrote the book that started this war." The bookplate is that of her husband.

Stowe.

Henry W. Taft
Engraver Tiffany and Co.
(Plate 29022)

Henry Waters Taft (1859—1945) was the brother of William Howard Taft, President of the United States succeeding Theodore Roosevelt. H. W. Taft was a distinguished anti-trust lawyer who investigated and prosecuted the Tobacco Trust. A lifelong Republican, he turned down an opportunity to work in the Roosevelt administration, but later was a supporter of The League of Nations. He was a member of the San Francisco Bohemian Club, as was his brother, and was a member of the Sons of the American Revolution. Among the awards he received was the Imperial Order of Meiji, 2nd Class Gold and Silver Star conferred by the Emperor of Japan.

Ellen Axson Wilson
Engraver Unknown
(Plate 24050)

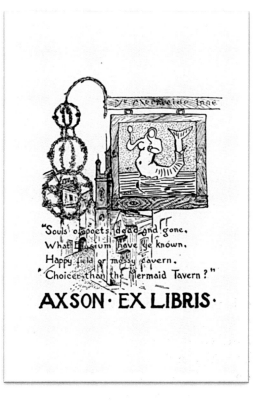

Ellen Axson (1860—1914) was Woodrow Wilson's first wife. He had known her since she was a child, and married her when she was 25 and he was 28. Together they had three daughters. They spent the first years in the White House together.

Ellen Axson had a liking for art, music and literature, and was an accomplished painter. She was a descendent of slave owners, and spent her time in the White House working for the betterment of black people in the Washington, D. C. area. She died of Bright's disease when she was 54. On her deathbed, she begged Wilson to marry again.

Woodrow Wilson
Engraver Unknown
(Plate 20020)

Woodrow Wilson
Engraver Carl S. Junge
(Plate 20026)

Woodrow Wilson (1856—1924) did marry again, to Edith Bolling, who was reputed to have made many of his decisions following his debilitating strokes while still in office.

Wilson's early career was as an academic, he had earned a Ph. D. from Johns Hopkins University, and later taught at and was the president of Princeton.

In public life, Wilson was an advocate for small businesses and farmers, proposed his famous "14 points" to achieve world peace at the Treaty of Versailles, and created the League of Nations. He is currently ranked by many presidential scholars as one of the top 10 Presidents of the United States, and was awarded the Nobel Peace Prize.

The 30th President of the United States was **Calvin Coolidge** (1872—1933), who also completed the final two years of Warren G Harding's presidency. Coolidge was credited with restoring the presidency to normalcy following Harding's Teapot Dome scandal, and several known sexual affairs. Calvin Coolidge was a Republican country lawyer who said little.

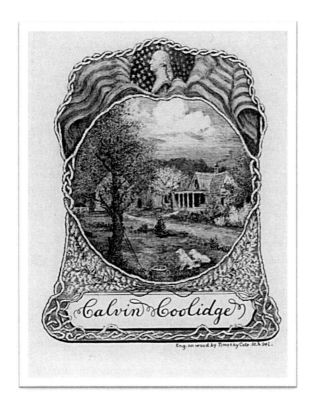

Calvin Coolidge
Engraved on Wood Timothy Cole
(Plate 20017)

While in the Massachusetts legislature, he voted in favor of women's suffrage and as President spoke in favor of civil rights for African Americans and Catholics. He signed the Indian Citizens Act which made U. S. citizens of all American Indians.

In what may be his most exciting speech titled "Have Faith in Massachusetts", Coolidge was quoted as saying "Expect to be called a stand patter, but don't be a stand patter. Expect to be called a demagogue but don't be a demagogue. Don't hesitate to be as revolutionary as science. Don't hesitate to be as reactionary as the multiplication table."

Herbert Hoover
Engraver Unknown
(Plate 20016)

Herbert Hoover (1874—1964) was born into a Quaker family. His training was as a mining engineer, and he spent several years in China and Africa practicing his trade and making several million dollars. While in China, both he and his wife learned Mandarin Chinese. He became Secretary of Commerce under Warren G. Harding and Calvin Coolidge, and followed the latter into the Presidency.

Unfortunately for everyone, in office less than 8 months, Hoover presided over the beginning of the Great Depression with the Wall Street Crash of 1929. His remedies involved big projects largely benefitting big businesses, but did little to reverse the downward spiral of the economy. During his life, Hoover wrote 16 books, engaged in national public life even after his Presidency, and strongly supported enforcement of prohibition. He was followed into office by Franklin Delano Roosevelt.

Franklin Delano Roosevelt (1882—1945) came into office at the beginning of the Great Depression and left (died) at the end of World War II 12 years later. The Japanese had brought the United States into the war with the bombing of Pearl Harbor on December 7, 1941.

Franklin Delano Roosevelt
Engraver Unknown
(Plate 20029)

The war ended after President Harry Truman, Roosevelt's Vice President, authorized the dropping of the atomic bomb on the Japanese cities of Hiroshima and Nagasaki.

During the war, Roosevelt signed an interment order that forced 100,000 Japanese Americans from their homes and put them in internment camps. Sixteen million men, many of Japanese origin, and 300,000 women were drafted or volunteered for military service during the war and by all accounts served the United States well.

Before December 7, 1941, President Roosevelt's greatest concern was ending the Great Depression. In his first 100 days, he instituted a program of recovery, reform and relief called the New Deal. It put millions of people back to work, fed millions of others, and restructured government and the American economy.

Eleanor Roosevelt
Engraver Dorothy Sturges Harding
(Plate 20030)

Eleanor Roosevelt (1884—1962) is the most highly respected and politically astute woman of 20th century American politics. President Truman called her the First Lady of the World in tribute to her activity and dedication to human rights. She guided and organized the United Nations "Universal Declaration of Human Rights", which still ranks as the most decent statement of human rights ever written. At the end of her term in the United Nations, Eleanor Roosevelt received a standing ovation from all the delegates, something no other ordinary delegate has received.

Eleanor became the eyes and legs of her husband who early in his life was crippled by polio. She had a great influence on his political agenda, but also pursued an agenda of her own, championing the rights of black people and inviting hundreds of African American guests to the White House. She was also politically active for other minorities, women's rights, and supported the need to help people around the world. When Marion Anderson was denied access to Constitution Hall by the Daughters of the American Revolution, Eleanor resigned her membership in the group and arranged for it to occur on the steps of the Lincoln Memorial. Even after Pearl Harbor, she spoke out against anti-Japanese prejudice and opposed her husband's internment order.

Franklin and Eleanor Roosevelt had six children, but Eleanor apparently didn't like sex and described it as an ordeal to be borne. Franklin, on the other hand, did like sex and carried on an affair with Lucy Mercer to the end of his life. Eleanor also liked women and was quite close to Amelia Earhart. Eleanor Roosevelt's funeral was attended by President Kennedy and former Presidents Eisenhower and Truman. Eleanor, Franklin and Theodore Roosevelt were featured in a 2014 Ken Burn's documentary on their lives and contributions to the United States and the world. Eleanor Roosevelt's bookplate was engraved by **Dorothy Sturgis Harding** (1891—1978), a New Englander, in 1935.

Chapter V: American Authors

Many of the most important American authors such as Faulkner and Hemingway are not included in this narrative because their bookplates were not found in the Blackburn Collection. However, several of those who were found had a photograph and/or autograph that Ida Mae and Oscar Taylor Blackburn saved along with their respective bookplates. Some autographs are also shown.

It would take an encyclopedia--and Wikipedia has been used extensively in this regard—to list all of the literary, musical and artistic works of these authors. Only a couple of examples have been included for each author, and occasionally a quotation or poem seemed appropriate. Many of these authors are now fairly obscure, but in their time they were highly recognized, and still have their place in American literature.

Fannie Hurst
Engraver N. W. Photographer Unknown
(Plate 23010)

Fannie Hurst (1889—1968) was an exceedingly prolific American novelist, short story and screen script writer. Although not much read today, she covered many social issues in her books including race relations, women's rights, public health and worker's rights, and the humane treatment of animals. A recurring theme in her books is the individual's struggle with social customs of a callous society. Several of her books and stories were made into movies, and she had 33 credits for screen and stage adaptations. Her most famous novel was *Imitation of Life* (1933) which dealt with race relations, in particular the difficulties encountered by mixed race women in a white dominated society. An extensive collection of her papers is housed at Brandeis University Special Collections section.

The children's books of **Anne Parrish** (1888—1957) were highly successful. She wrote twenty books including *The Perennial Bachelor* and *The Dream Coach*. Anne Parrish's mother was a friend of the expressionist artist, Mary Cassatt. Anne's sister was an artist and writer, and her cousin was the engraver and artist Maxfield Parrish, a few of whose bookplates are found in the Blackburn Collection. Anne Parrish studied art under Thomas Eakins but decided to pursue a career in writing instead. She also collected art, one of her pieces being "Monet Painting in his Garden at Argenteuil" by Renoir.

Anne Parrish
Engraver Unknown Photographer Unknown
(Plate 23012)

Natalie Sumner Lincoln
Engraver Unknown
(Plate 23021)

Natalie Sumner Lincoln (1881—1935) was born and lived in Washington, D.C. where she wrote romance and murder mystery novels. Among her books still available are *The Cat's Paw, The Red Seal, I Spy,* and *The Moving Finger.* Others of her 22 novels can be found in Project Gutenberg.

Mary Johnston (1870—1936) was an American southern novelist who wrote historical fiction. Among her books were *Prisoners of Hope* and *To Have and To Hold* set in colonial times. *The Goddess of Reason* used the French Revolution as its backdrop, and *The Long Roll* was about the American Civil War. Johnston was criticized by Anna Jackson, wife of Stonewall Jackson, for her portrayals of Confederate soldiers in *The Long Roll*. Whereas most novels of the time tended to glorify and romanticize the Confederate south, Johnston presented an anti-war message that shied away from the racist portrayals of Reconstruction. Mary Johnston was an early advocate for women's rights and suffrage.

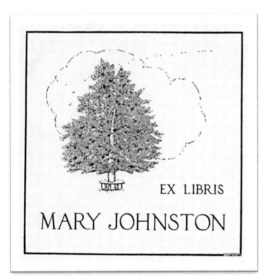

*Mary Johnston
Engraver and
Photographer
Unknown (Plate
23028)*

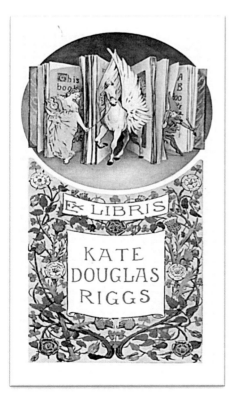

*Kate Douglas
Wiggin
Engraver and
Photographer
Unknown
(Plate 23030)*

Kate Douglas Wiggin aka **Kate Douglas Riggs** (1856—1923) was married twice. She was an early proponent of sending children to kindergarten, and started the first free kindergarten in the San Francisco slums in 1878 and well as established a training school for kindergarten teachers. By chance, at 11 years of age, she rode on a train with Charles Dickens during his tour of America, and had an extensive conversation with him which may have begun her interest in a writing career. She wrote of her conversation with Dickens in "A Child's Journey with Dickens." She was mainly the author of children's books, twenty in all, including the classic novel *Rebecca of Sunnybrook Farm*. *The Story of Patsy* and *The Bird's Christmas Carol* were two of her other books.

Vincent Starrett
Engraver Fridolf Johnson
(Plate 24001)

His name given at birth was **Charles Vincent Emerson Starrett** (1886—1974). Although born in Canada, he moved to Chicago to become a newspaperman with the Chicago Daily News and in 1915, he covered the Mexican war for the newspaper. During his career, he wrote poetry, novels and movie scripts. First editions of his books are highly collectable, and retail for high prices in antiquarian book stores.

Much of Starrett's fame, however, came from his interest in Sherlock Holmes as indicated by his bookplate (24001). Early on, he wrote "The Adventure of the Unique 'Hamlet'" which had Sherlock Holmes in possession of a missing copy of the play with inscription by the bard himself. Another Starrett book is *The Private Life of Sherlock Holmes* which one critic called "The greatest book about Sherlock Holmes ever written."

Vincent Starrett
Engraver Unknown
(Plate 24002)

Starrett called himself at various times the "Number One American Bookman" and "a damned fool about books". He was an avid book collector. Two other books he wrote were biographies of Ambrose Bierce and Steven Crane, both of whom also wrote books about the American Civil War.

A Sherlockian sonnet by Starrett is called "221 B" for 221 Baker Street, Sherlock Holmes fictional residence:

"Here dwell together two men of note
Who never lived and so can never die:
How very near they seem yet how remote
That age before the world went all awry.

But still the game's afoot for those with ears
Attuned to catch the distant halloo:
England is England yet, for all our fears—
Only those things the heart believes are true.

A yellow fog swirls past the window pane
As night descends upon this fabled street:
A lonely hansom splashes through the rain,
The ghostly gas lamps fail at twenty feet.

Here, though the world explode, these two survive,
And it is always eighteen ninety-five."

From the Library of
Robert Louis Stevenson
AT VAILIMA

Robert Louis Balfour Stevenson (1850—1894) was born in Scotland but spent much of his time in America and married an American wife. His last residence was at Vailima, Samoa where he is buried with the inscription on his tomb at Mount Vaea, "Home is the sailor, home from the sea, and the hunter home from the hill" taken from his poem. The signature on the plate, Isohe Shony, is unknown, but she may have been Stevenson's literary executor.

By some counts, Stevenson is the 26th most translated English language author, ahead even of Oscar Wilde and Edgar Allen Poe. His writing was admired by fellow authors Marcel Proust, Bertolt Brecht, Arthur Conan Doyle, Henry James, Ernest Hemingway, Rudyard Kipling, Jack London, Vladimir Nabokov, James Barrie, and C.K. Chesterton and millions of kids the world over but not by literary critics and he was generally excluded from anthologies of English and American literature.

Stevenson wrote 13 novels, 22 short stories and 123 musical compositions. His best known novels are *Treasure Island, Kidnapped,* and *The Strange Case of Dr. Jekyll and Mr. Hyde* but he also wrote *The*

Black Arrow: A Tale of Two Roses, *The Master of Ballantrae*, and *Weir of Hermiston* which was unfinished at the time of his death.

Althea Paine, Literary Executor
Samuel Langhorne Clemens Library
Engraver Unknown
(Plate 24009)

Both **Samuel Langhorne Clemens** (1835—1910) aka **Mark Twain**--and Bret Harte visited the gold fields of California at Angels Camp and wrote stories set in the region. Twain's story, "The Celebrated Jumping Frog of Calaveras County" is immensely popular, and was immediately translated into other languages including Greek when it first appeared.

This volume is from the Library of

SAMUEL LANGHORNE CLEMENS

(Mark Twain)

Althea Bigelow Paine

Literary Executor

Sold February, 1911, by The Anderson Auction Company,
No. 12 East 46th Street, New York.

The story became the basis for an annual Jumping Frog contest celebration in Angels Camp (see below a bookplate of Loring Gary Calkins that also references Angels Camp). The plate is signed by **Albert Bigelow Paine**, Twain's literary executor and biographer.

Samuel Langhorne Clemens grew up in Hannibal, Missouri, the site of his two most famous novels, *The Adventures of Tom Sawyer* (1876), and *The Adventures of Huckleberry Finn* (1883). Another book, *Life on the Mississippi* records Twain's early life as a river boat captain.

Clemens traveled widely, became a friend to presidents, industrialists, artists and European Royalty, and achieved enormous fame as a lecturer, writer and humorist. William Faulkner called Mark Twain "the father of American literature" and *Huckleberry Finn* is often referred to as the "great American novel." Clemens wife was a socialite named Olivia Langdon. Through her, he met abolitionists, "socialists, principled atheists, and activists for women's rights and social equality."

Twain's lectures and humor often express a biting commentary on politics, equality, racism, and other social issues. He supported the abolition of slavery and emancipation of slaves, and reversed himself on the question of imperialism by becoming at the end of his life an ardent anti-imperialist opposing the annexation of the Philippines by the United States. Among his controversial statements about religion, Mark Twain said "If our Maker is all-powerful for good or for evil, He is not in his right mind."

Bret Harte (1839—1902) was born in the Eastern United States, his grandfather being an orthodox Jewish immigrant who helped found the New York Stock Exchange. Harte's education ended when he was 13, but he soon took up writing through journalism. As a reporter, Bret Harte covered the massacre of the Wiyot Indians in Humboldt County, California for San Francisco and New York papers.

Bret Harte
Engraver Unknown
(Plate 24070)

A group of white vigilante men attacked and killed from 80 to 200 Wiyot women and children—most of the men of the tribe happened to be away—using clubs, hatchets and machetes so that gunshots wouldn't be heard. A single survivor lived to tell the story. Harte was sickened by what he saw, and had his life threatened for writing the story.

Bret Harte gained literary fame by writing stories about mining towns. "The Luck of Roaring Camp" is about a baby boy raised by gold miners after his mother died in childbirth; they thought the baby boy brought them luck. Good luck didn't play in "The Outcasts of Poker Flat" where a number of sinful people including a card shark were forced to leave Poker Flat in the winter and perished. Another Harte story called "The Stolen Cigar Case" with a character named Hemlock Jones is a parody of Sherlock Holmes. Mark Twain and Bret Harte are highly regarded in California history. No less than twenty-seven localities are named after them, including Bret Harte High School, Twain Harte community, and the town of Angels Camp.

The Players West Room
Engraved by Loring Gary Calkins
(Plate 50081)

Loring Gary Calkins' (1887—1960) description of "The Players West-Room" bookplate related that:

"the dominating subject…is the sculptured bust of Edwin Booth, founder of the Players Club of New York. The bust was made by Launt Thompson of Edwin Booth as a young man in the costume of Hamlet. The Circle indicates eternity, his fame having no end. The masks of Tragedy and Comedy are carved on a plaque on the door of the Players West Room, Los Angeles. The lower panel depicts the old theatre at Angels Camp, California, where Booth is thought to have first played Hamlet in this crude gold mining camp." Mark Twain was associated with Booth as founder of The Players.

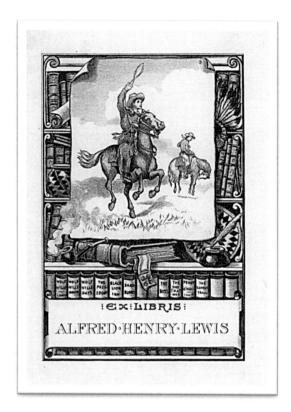

Alfred Henry Lewis
Engraver Frederick Remington
(Plate 25077)

Alfred Henry Lewis (1855—1914) was an investigative journalist, lawyer, novelist, editor and short story writer. Although much of his career was spent in journalism—he wrote about corruption in New York politics, a life of Andrew Jackson, and other muckraking pieces—he also wrote short stories and western novels. Available through Project Gutenberg are *Faro Nell and Her Friends: Wolfville Stories*, *How the Raven Died*, and *The Sunset Trail*.

Lewis' bookplate was one of three designed by **Frederick Remington**. Remington is known for his realistic depictions of western "cowboy and Indian" life. His sculptures are copied and sold in curio shops and western art stores.

An American poet and contemporary of Mark Twain (Samuel Clemens) with whom he traveled and performed at one point in his career, **James Whitcomb Riley** (1849—1916) was one of a very few poets to become wealthy from his writing and performances. His association with Mark Twain was short, though, because Riley was the more popular performer. One reviewer wrote Clemens "shriveled up into a bitter patch of melancholy in the fierce light of Mr. Riley's humor."

James Whitcomb Riley
Engraver Unknown
(Plate 33039)

Riley is most famous for having written "Little Orphan Annie" and "The Raggedy Man." He once created a scandal by writing a poem imitating Edgar Allen Poe's style and publishing it as a new-found Poe poem. Uncovered, his and his paper's reputations suffered.

Another problem involving Riley stemmed from his alcohol addiction; once he failed to perform because he was too drunk, which in Victorian times became a highly scandalous, but publishable story. Riley wrote a thousand poems during his lifetime, many of them children's poems and many of them written in 'dialect'. In part, he made a living giving readings or performances of his poetry, and for a season toured with Mark Twain but—as the story goes—Twain didn't

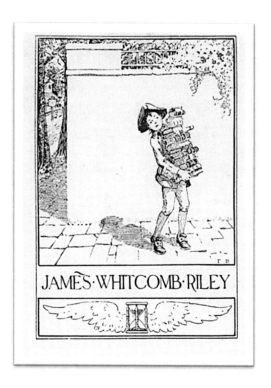

like being upstaged or outperformed by Riley and terminated the relationship. A reviewer wrote, "Clemens shriveled up unto a bitter patch of melancholy in the fierce light of Mr. Riley's humor."

Riley once wrote a poem imitating Edgar Allen Poe's style, and published it as Poe's. The hoax was discovered, and both Riley's and his publisher's reputation suffered. Another scandal caused by Riley occurred once when he was too drunk to go on stage and the straight-laced press made a story of it.

Rupert Hughes
Engraver Unknown
(Plate 24020)

Rupert Hughes (1872—1956) was a novelist, screenwriter and short story writer. He wrote 11 novels and a significant 3 volume biography of George Washington, several stage plays and scripts for films. His first novel, *The Whirlwind*, was set in the Civil War era, and may have been based on his father's war experiences. Hughes, himself, served in the military, his regiment being one of the groups assigned to capture Poncho Villa. Another of Hughes books was titled *Love Affairs of Great Musicians*.

Hughes, also, was a composer, and wrote several songs for his plays, one which was a Broadway musical. During his life, Hughes wrote over a hundred short stories. Rupert Hughes was the uncle of the billionaire, Howard Hughes.

John Erskine
Engraver Unknown
(Plate 24021)

An educator, author, pianist, composer, **John Erskine** (1879—1951) was an English professor at Amherst College and Columbia University. While at Amherst, he wrote an essay called "The Moral Obligation to be Intelligent" (1915), and started a 'core curriculum' project while teaching at Columbia that later became the Great Books of the Western World project. During his life, Erskine wrote over a

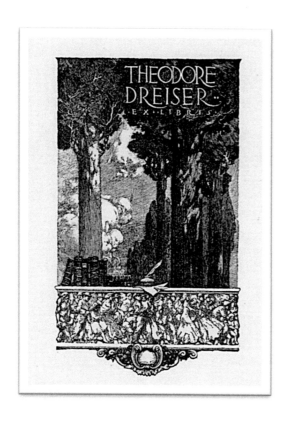

hundred books including *The Private Life of Helen of Troy* that became the basis of several cinema and theatrical productions. John Erskine was the first president of the Julliard School of Music, and he composed and contributed to several operatic and other musical scores.

Theodore Dreiser
Engraver Unknown
(Plate 24031)

Theodore Herman Albert Dreiser (1871—1945) was the twelfth of thirteen kids. His brother was Paul Dresser who became a Tin Pan Alley performer and actor and composer of over 150 songs, two of them being "On the Banks of the Wabash" and "Far Away". Theodore Dreiser wrote a biography of his brother, and published ten novels together with thirteen other books. Two of his novels, *Sister Carrie* and *An American Tragedy* are considered American classics. Both have young women as characters who fall into bad circumstances as their central theme.

In his earlier life, Theodore Dreiser was a journalist of some note, interviewing and writing about several well-known personages of his day. Dreiser's mother was a Mennonite who married a Roman catholic which caused her to be disowned by her family. An irony of Dreiser's life was that he planned to travel from Europe to America on the Titanic, but was talked out of it by a publisher who wanted him to take a less expensive boat.

James Branch Cabell
Engraver Unknown
(Plate 24032)

An early writer of fantasy fiction, **James Branch Cabell** (1879—1958) was highly regarded by writers such as H. L. Mencken, Mark Twain and Sinclair Lewis. Although given credit for influencing later fantasy writers, Cabell is mostly forgotten today. His most well-known novel is *Jürgen, A Comedy of Justice* in which the main character of the book—a scoundrel—spends a lot of time traveling around seducing local women including the Devils wife.

Jürgen got the attention of the New York Society for the Suppression of Vice who took Cabell to court, but he wasn't convicted.

Cabell was born in Virginia, and attended college at William and Mary from which he was dismissed because of an "intimate relationship" with one of his professors. He later returned and graduated. In 1901, Cabell published his first short stories, and he was accused of murder of his mother's lover, one John Scott, a wealthy citizen of Richmond. The scandal passed, and he went on to write 52 books including a 25 volume novel called the *Biography of Manuel* that takes place through several generations of his character's lives.

Booth Tarkington
Engraver Unknown
(Plate 24038)

Booth Tarkington (1869—1946) was a highly popular novelist whose works became the subject of several film adaptations by productions of Orson Wells. Booth Tarkington, William Faulkner and John Updike are the only persons to receive more than one Pulitzer Prize for Fiction. Tarkington, who never graduated from college, attended Purdue University for a short time and Princeton University where he met and became lifelong friends with Woodrow Wilson. Both universities subsequently awarded Tarkington honorary doctorate degrees as did several others during his life.

Booth Tarkington's best known novel is *The Magnificent Ambersons*, one of a trilogy of novels set in the period between the Civil War and the early 20ᵗʰ Century. Several of Tarkington's literary works have become the basis for movies.

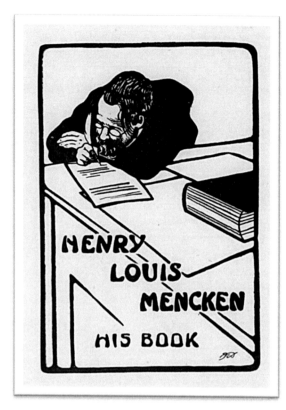

Henry Louis Mencken, aka H. L. Mencken (1880—1956) had an acid tongue that he used with relish pursuing a career as a journalist, essayist, satirist, critic of American life. He wrote three dozen books, many of which are still in print, and a multi-volume study of the English Language as it is spoken in America. Mencken's favorite book was *The Adventures of Huckleberry Finn*.

The writers for Wikipedia wrote that Mencken was "skeptical of economic theories and particularly critical of anti-intellectualism, bigotry, populism, fundamentalist Christianity, creationism, organized religion, the existence of God, and osteopathic/chiropractic medicine." Mencken invented the phrase 'Monkey Trial' to describe the Scopes trial about evolution that was defended by Clarence Darrow.

Mencken married, but he once called marriage 'the end of hope' and democracy 'the worship of jackals by jackasses'. In 1931, the Arkansas legislature passed a motion to pray for H. L. Mencken's soul after he had called the state the "apex of moronia".

Three trials in which **Clarence Darrow** (1857—1938) was the lawyer for the defense captivated Americans, the Sweet Trial which was about race, the Massie Trial which was about revenge, and the Scopes Trial about bigotry and evolution. Clarence Darrow was a leading member of the American Civil Liberties Union. In the third trial (1925), Darrow's legal opponent was William Jennings Bryant, a

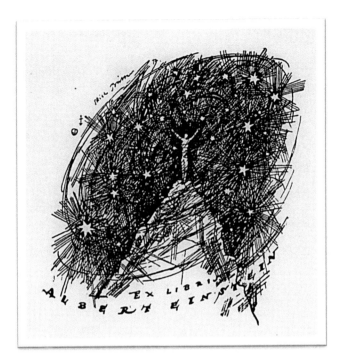

three time candidate for President of the United States and one of the most gifted orators of his time.

Several books, movies, television programs and songs have been written about Clarence Darrow and/or the Scopes 'Monkey' trial, the most famous being Spencer Tracy's movie *Inherit the Wind* (1960). Darrow's own writing including seven books by himself and another eight biographies are housed at the University of Minnesota.

Albert Einstein
Engraver Erick Buttner
(Plate 27004)

Likely the most celebrated writer of the 20th Century was a scientist, **Albert Einstein** (1879—1955) whose famous equation $E=mc^2$ or the theory of mass—energy equivalence is one of the two most recognizable mathematical equations in the world (the Pythagorean Theorem $a^2+b^2=c^2$ is the other).

Einstein's bookplate was created by a German painter **Erich Buttner** (1889—1936) supposedly based on some doodling of Einstein's. Among the several astounding theories Einstein pursued were the *Special Theory of Relativity* (1905) and the *General Theory of Relativity* (1907 and 1915). He spent much of his time thinking of how to unify the two, but this work was not completed.

The *Special Theory of Relativity* (1905) posited that the speed of light was independent of the motion of the observer, which led to several impressive 'mind experiments' such as imagining 'a train traveling at the speed of light...' His law of the photoelectric effect anticipated Quantum Theory and understanding the motion of molecules.

The *General Theory of Relativity* theorized that gravity can 'bend light' resulting in the warping of space—time because of gravitational attraction of masses. This led to an understanding that 'black holes' are regions of the universe where the gravitational attraction is so strong that even light cannot escape.

Albert Einstein was awarded the Nobel Prize for Physics in 1921. One of his talents was playing the violin; among his favorite composers were Mozart and Beethoven. During his life, he campaigned for civil rights, and joined the NAACP to combat "America's worst disease." Just about everything Einstein said or wrote has become a quotable statement. A personal favorite is "We cannot solve our problems with the same [level of] thinking we used when we created them."

Bennett A. Cerf
Engraver Rockwell Kent
(Plate 24042)

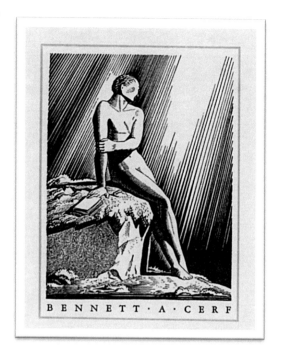

Bennett Cerf (1898—1971) was one of the founders of Random House, a book publisher that was known for the quality of its books. Cerf sued the government, "United States vs One Small Book Ulysses" over censorship. He won the landmark case, and later published James Joyce's *Ulysses* in the United States.

Bennett Cerf's father was a lithographer who married a tobacco heiress. Bennett Cerf was famous for his humor and puns, and appeared regularly on television in "What's My Line". He also wrote 14 books himself. His bookplate was designed and sculpted by Rockwell Kent.

William H Prescott
Engraver Unknown
(Plate 24056)

Among the books written by **William H. Prescott** (1796—1859) are the *History of the Reign of Ferdinand and Isabella the Catholic* (1837), the *History of the Conquest of Mexico* (1843), and the *History of the Conquest of Peru* (1847). Prescott is respected for his used of original and authoritative sources, for his scholarship and meticulous sourcing of material, and for his propensity to include bibliographical citations and critical notes in his books.

Prescott, Arizona and the Colegio Anglo Americano Prescott in Arequipa, Peru are named after him.

86

Hamlin Garland
Engraver Isabel Garland Lord
(Plate 24066)

Hamlin Garland's (1860—1940) bookplate was designed and printed by his daughter. Hannibal Hamlin Garland was a novelist, short story writer, biographer, and later in his life, a psychic researcher. Born in Wisconsin, Garland grew up in the mid-west, and traveled widely, finally ending up in California.

In 1922, Garland was awarded a Pulitzer Prize for *A Daughter of the Middle Border*. Among his most read books—he published 38 fiction books including volumes of short stories, 4 biographical books, and 4 volumes of *Memoirs*—are *Main Traveled Roads* and *The Trail of the Gold Seekers*. The latter was based on his experiences with the Yukon Gold Rush.

Jack London
Engraver Ernest James Cross
(Plate 24067)

Jack London's (1876—1916) (born John Griffith Chaney) stories are based on his experiences in San Francisco where he was born, Alaska where he unsuccessfully sought a fortune in the Klondike gold rush, and on the sea. He won an early writing contest by describing his nearly fatal first sea voyage at 17 that took place in a hurricane.

His most famous books are *The Call of the Wild*, *White Fang*, *Martin Eden* and *The Sea-Wolf*. *The Sea-Wolf* has been adapted for cinema no less than 13 times. Wikipedia reports that "London's intention in writing *The Sea-Wolf* was an attack on (Nietzsche's) superman philosophy".

87

Charmian Kittredge (1871—1955) was Jack London's second wife. She wrote three books herself—*Our Hawaii, The Log of the Snark,* and a biography called *The Book of Jack London.*

Charmian (Kittredge) London's bookplate was sculpted by an Australian woodcut artist, **L. Roy Davies** who was born in 1897 and died in 1979. His artwork is highly collectable.

Oliver Wendell Holmes Sr. (1809—1894) was a physician, poet, author and professor. He attended and taught at Dartmouth and Harvard College. Before he died, he gave his 900 volume library to the Boston Medical Library which included books ranging over four centuries.

Oliver Wendell Holmes
Engraver Unknown
(Plate 24071)

Oliver Wendell Holmes, Sr. wrote a poem called "Old Ironsides" that led to the preservation of the USS Constitution, a Navy frigate that still is the oldest warship afloat.

Another of Holmes' poems was "The Cocked Hat" which Edgar Allen Poe called "one of the finest poems in the English language' and a poem Abraham Lincoln used to recite often. Holmes said the poem was inspired by the last remaining participant of the Boston Tea Party.

Oliver Wendell Holmes wrote novels, articles, biographies, medical studies, poetry, and "table-talk books'. He also was the father of the American Supreme Court justice, Oliver Wendell Holmes, Jr.

Holmes' bookplate is called the Nautical Bookplate. Holmes' made many contributions to medicine, one of them being the word, anesthesia, which meant insensibility of touch to objects. He correctly predicted the word would be used the world over.

Eugene Field
Engraver Unknown
(Plate 24075)

Eugene Field (1850—1895) began his career as a journalist in St. Louis, Missouri and later for the Chicago Daily News. His father was a lawyer who represented Dred Scott, a slave who sued for his freedom. The case was sometimes called the lawsuit that started the Civil War.

Eugene Field studied law, but found it didn't appeal to him. He wrote a dozen books of poetry primarily for children, including the poem "Wynken, Blynken and Nod." Some of his literary works were illustrated by Mayfield Parrish.

Robert Frost
Engraver J. J. Lankes
(Plate 33005)

Robert Frost's (1874—1963) poetry is studied nearly by every grade school and high school student in America. Frost was born in San Francisco, but soon moved to Massachusetts where he attended Dartmouth and Harvard universities and although he never received a college degree, he was awarded over 40 honorary degrees during his lifetime.

John F. Kennedy selected Frost to read a poem, "The Gift Outright" at his inaugural in 1960, three years before Frost's death. Frost received a Congressional Gold Medal for Poetry in 1960, and is still one of the most popular and critically acclaimed poets of the 20th century. He won four Pulitzer prizes for his work.

Frost's bookplate was engraved by **J. J. Lankes** (1884—1960) who was a life-long friend and illustrator of many of Frost's books. J. J. Lankes bookplates and other woodcuts are held and exhibited by 17 major museums and universities including the Metropolitan Museum of Art in New York City, NY and the Congressional Library in Washington, D. C.

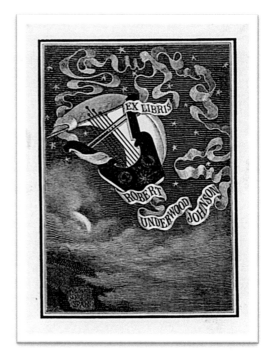

Robert Underwood Johnson
Engraver Unknown
(Plate 33011)

Although not a major figure in American literature, **Robert Underwood Johnson** (1853—1937) published 9 books of poetry and two books about history, including *Battles and Leaders of the Civil War.* He is said to have persuaded Ulysses S. Grant to write his *Memoirs*, and along with naturalist John Muir, was a driving force leading to the establishment of Yosemite National Park, and later the creation of the Sierra Club. Also a diplomat, Johnson was decorated by the French and Italian governments for his contributions and diplomacy.

Chapter VI: Stage, Cinema and Music

Ignaz Jan Paderewski (1860—1941) is known for having been a composer and pianist, but he also played a large part in Polish independence. During the 1919 Paris Peace Conference, he convinced President Wilson that Polish independence should be one of Wilson's 14 Points. Paderewski's political career included serving as a Prime Minister and Foreign Minister of Poland.

Ignaz Jan Paderewski
Engraver W.P.P.
(Plate 33008)

Ignaz Jan Paderewski's lasting international legacy is, however, as a musician. He began piano lessons at age 12, made his musical debut at age 27, and became hugely popular throughout Europe and eventually the United States, especially with young women who flocked to his concerts. He played to full houses at Madison Square Garden which seats 20,000 and Carnegie Hall. He also appeared in a 1936 film about his life called *Moonlight Sonata.*

Among the pieces he wrote for piano was the Minuet in G, Opus 14/1. His only opera was *Manu* in 1901 that was performed at the Metropolitan Opera and still is the only Polish opera written by a Polish composer to be performed there. His last piece was *Symphony in B Minor* (1909) that is 75 minutes long.

Jessica Dragonette
Engraver E. B. Bird
(Plate 33036)

Jessica Dragonette (1900—1980) was born in India, but became an orphan at an early age. She was raised in a convent, where she received voice lessons that led to a career in music as a soprano singing operetta and semi-classical music. In 1926 and thereafter for 22 years she began singing on the radio, and was voted the best female singer in the United States in 1942 and 1943. During those years, she did innumerable charity performances for War Bonds, and performed for troops which earned her an honorary military designation as a Colonel. She also sang in an animated picture of *Gulliver's Travels.*

Jessica Dragonette's bookplate was sculpted by **Elisha Brown Bird** (1868—1943) who is recognized as one of the masters of bookplate engraving, and was the President of the American Society of Bookplate Collectors and Engravers for many years. Many of Bird's bookplates are 'artistic' insofar as they represent the character of the purchaser in their design as shown by the music and performer motifs in Dragonets' plate.

Richard Strauss
Engraver Unknown
(Plate 33009)

Besides being one of the most prolific composers of the 20th century, **Richard Strauss** (1864—1949) is still one of the most often performed composers, with only Puccini operas being performed more frequently. His 40 plus major musical pieces include operas, symphonies, violin and piano concertos, and solo works for horn, piano, horns, oboe, bassoon, and clarinet.

Among the most famous of his operas are *Die Rosenkavalier* and *Salome* based on a play by Oscar Wilde. Most movie goers in the world have heard some of *Thus Spoke Zarathustra* that was used as background music in the science fiction movie *2001*. Strauss has been called the greatest composer in the first half of the 20th century, and during his lifetime was recognized as a prominent conductor.

Enrico Caruso
Engraver A. N. Macdonald
(Plate 33043)

Still the most recognized tenor in the world (Pavarotti notwithstanding), **Enrico Caruso** (1873—1921) almost single handedly brought Italian opera to most of the listening world. During his relatively short career from 1902--1920 Caruso released 290 commercial recordings that are still available on CDs and through digital downloads. He made 863 appearances at the New York Metropolitan Opera, and sang at La Scala in Italy, the Royal Opera House in London, Covent Garden in London, the Mariinsky Theater in St. Petersburg, and the Teatro Colon in Buenos Aires.

Enrico Caruso was born in Naples. His father, who was a mechanic and foundry worker, thought his son should also become a foundry worker and started him

in an apprenticeship at age 11. Fortunately for opera lovers, Caruso liked singing more than foundry work, and began to earn a living giving street concerts. After voice lessons, he had his professional stage debut at age 22, and went on to make millions of dollars through performances and recordings released by RCA. He appeared in two motion pictures, the first ironically being a silent film.

Caruso had four children by a married mistress of 11 years, and after marriage to a younger woman another daughter. He smoked heavily, had bronchitis and died from complications of pleurisy and empyema at age 48. His funeral was attended by thousands.

Enrico Caruso's bookplate was engraved by **Arthur Nelson MacDonald** (1866—1940) who was a silver engraver who created nearly four hundred bookplates as well as other book illustrations during his career, and is acknowledged to be among the most highly respected engravers of his time along with E.D. French, J.W. Spenceley and Sidney L. Smith.

The premier of Puccini's *La fanciulla del West* with Enrico Caruso and Emmy Destinn singing the lead roles under the direction of conductor Arturo Toscanini took place in 1910 at the New York Metropolitan Opera House.

Emmy Destinn
Engraver Unknown
(Plate 21041)

Emmy Destinn (1878—1930) was a Czech operatic soprano who began her music career studying violin, but changed once she became aware of the range and quality of her voice. She was already an operatic superstar by age 19, and during her career sang in 54 operas including 12 premiers, one of them being *Salome*, and another a premier of *Madame Butterfly* also with Caruso. She sung leading roles in *Aida*, *Carmen* and *Il Travatore*.

Emmy Destinn's biographers report that she was a poet, novelist and playwright as well as opera star. She has an asteroid, 6583 Destinn, named after her, and her likeness appears on the 2000 Czech Koruna banknote.

David Garrick
Engraver Unknown
(Plate 21017)

David Garrick (1716—1779) was a Shakespearean actor, playwright, and the manager of the Theatre Royal in Drury Lane. He was especially famous for his realistic portrayals of King Richard III; William Hogarth did a painting of Garrick as Richard III. In 1769, Garrick staged a Shakespeare Jubilee at Stratford-upon-Avon. Garrick was a great friend of Samuel Johnson.

In 1831, the Garrick Club was established in his name, and had in its membership Dickens, Thackeray, Collins, Yates, Trollope, Barrie, Gilbert, and Pinero to name a few. Today, The Garrick Club has over 1300 performing artist members.

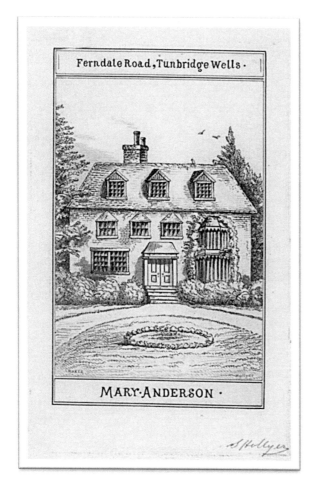

Mary Anderson
Engraver S. Hollyer
(Plate 21042)

Mary Antoinette Anderson (1859—1940) was a stage actress who also became known as Mary Anderson de Navarro in ten silent films. She began her career and Macaulay's Theatre playing Juliet in Louisville, Kentucky where her father had been enlisted in the Confederate States Army during the American Civil War. Mary Anderson had a successful stage career both in the United States and in England, where for several seasons she appeared at Stratford-upon-Avon in Shakespearean roles.

Samuel Hollyer (1825—1919), the engraver of Mary Anderson's bookplate, according to his obituary was one of the old school line engravers, a technique that was largely supplanted by photo engraving in the early 20th century. Among his most famous engravings is "Charles Dickens in his Study" and a series of 100 engravings of old New York that were given to the City in his will. Several Hollyer plates were found in the Blackburn Collection.

Howard Pyle (1853—1911) designed The Players Club bookplate (1894), and asked **Edwin Davis French** to engrave it, which he did. Pyle said to Edith Kermit Roosevelt "I think Mr. French is the best engraver in the world" although French wasn't able to engrave her plate.

Howard Pyle was an illustrator, artist, teacher and author who had several of the Wyeth family of artists as his students. He primarily illustrated children's books, medieval scenes, and pirate motifs. He is credited for creating the stereotypical dress of a pirate. Vincent Van Gogh, a contemporary of Pyle's, thought Pyle's art was incredibly good. An exhaustive set of Pyle's work is housed at the Helen Farr Sloan Library at the Delaware Art Museum, in Wilmington, Delaware.

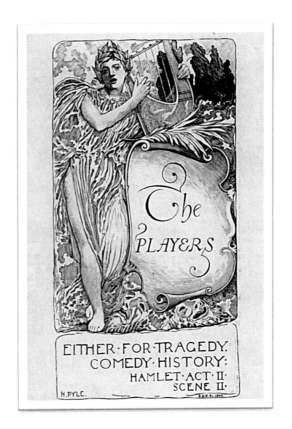

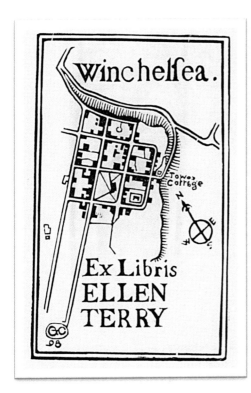

Alice Ellen Terry
Engraver Unknown
(Plate 21026)

Alice Ellen Terry (1847—1928) was for several years Britain's greatest Shakespearean actress. She was born into a family of theatre people; her parents and brothers and sisters were performers and/or theatre managers, etc. Her sister Kate, an actress herself who often played with Ellen, was the grandmother of the English actor, Sir John Gielgud. Ellen created several roles for Shakespeare's plays, among them Portia in *The Merchant of Venice* and Beatrice in *Much Ado About Nothing*. Besides Shakespeare's plays, she acted in most of the contemporary productions of her day including *The School for Scandal* and *The Admirable Creighton*.

Ellen Terry was married three times, had several extra-marital liaisons that produced two of her children, and carried on a famous letter correspondence with George Bernard Shaw.

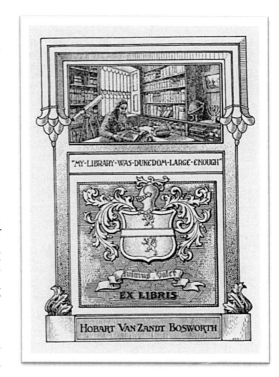

Hobart Van Zandt Bosworth (1867—1943) was a Hollywood actor, director, producer, and screen writer who by the end of his career had participated in large and small ways in 55 movies. His Hollywood career came after a number of years as a stage actor, appearing first as a stage manager for the California Theatre in San Francisco where he moved into Shakespearean acting in *Measure for Measure, Cymbeline, As You Like It* and others. He co-wrote a version of *Faust* that was staged for twenty years. After moving to Hollywood, Bosworth started his own company that made 31 movies bridging the silent film to talking movies period.

The writers of Wikipedia report that Bosworth was "a direct descendant of Miles Standish and John and Priscilla Alden on his father's side, and of New York's Van Zandt family, the first Dutch settlers to land in the New World on his mother's side," a lineage of which he was quite proud. As a young boy, Bosworth went to sea as a cabin boy for 3 years aboard the clipper ship *Sovereign of the Seas*, ending up in California.

Lawrence Barrett
Engraver Unknown
(Plate 21043)

The son of a poor tailor, **Lawrence Barrett** (1838—1891) served in the Massachusetts army in the American Civil War, but wasn't in any major battles. By 1853 he appeared in his first play, *The French Spy*, and had his first appearance in New York in 1856. As a Shakespearean actor, he performed as Hamlet, King Lear, Macbeth, Shylock, Richard III and as Richelieu and David Garrick in other plays. He spent several seasons in London, acting in the first production of *The Duchess of Padua*. Barrett worked for several years with Edmund Booth.

Helena (Modjeska) Modrzejewska
Engraver Unknown
(Plate 21024)

Helena Modjeska (1840—1909)--her spelling of her name used when appearing before English-speaking audiences--was a very prominent Polish stage actress who achieved success as a tragedian in Europe and the United States. After being the acknowledged reigning diva in the Polish theatre for ten years, she immigrated to the United States where she made her debut at the California theatre in San Francisco in 1877.

After acting in California for a time, she decided Modjeska decided that her English needed improvement and went to England for three years, after which she returned to America as a leading interpreter of nine tragic roles of Shakespeare, including Juliet and Ophelia. She produced and acted in Ibsen's *A Doll's House* which premiered in Louisville, Kentucky. She appeared and traveled with Lawrence Barrett and Edmund Booth.

Helena Modrzejewska's parentage is somewhat uncertain. It is believed her mother had an affair with Prince Wladyslaw Sanzuszko, a 13th generation member of the noble Sanzuszko line that began in 1443. The Sanzuszko family became famous for its collections of Arabian horses from the Slavista stud and for Persian carpets known as Sanguszko carpets.

Helena was godmother to actress Ethel Barrymore, and may have been the character model for Irene Adler, the only woman whom Sherlock Holmes ever loved in *A Scandal in Bohemia*. Several places are named after her, and Helena appears in several fiction and non-fiction books.

John Wilkes Booth
Photographer Unknown
(Plate 20015)

John Wilkes Booth (1838—1865) was the brother of Edwin Booth and the son of Junius Brutus Booth, all three successful Shakespearean actors. John Wilkes Booth debuted in *King Richard III*, and was acclaimed by the New York Herald as a 'veritable sensation' in that role.

His story is a little obscure, but popular history has it that he was a Confederate secret agent who supported slavery, and who had joined the No-Nothing Party. Booth's favorite line from *Richard III* was "I am determined to be a villain" which, unfortunately, he achieved for all time by being the assassin of President Lincoln.

97

Douglas Fairbanks (1883—1939) met **Mary Pickford** (1893—1979) in 1917 and they married in 1920 after dissolving prior marriages. At the time, she was the highest paid actress in Hollywood; during their marriage, the two of them were the most famous names in American show business, often regarded as 'royalty' of show business, and because of their business acumen, likely the richest.

He was born Douglas Elton Thomas Ullman in Denver, Colorado. His father was a lawyer, and helped found an early predecessor of the American Bar Association. Together, along with their friend Charlie Chaplin, the Fairbanks helped found United Artists, and The Motion Picture Academy of Arts and Sciences of which Douglas was the first president. Douglas Fairbanks hosted the first Academy Awards in 1929.

In later years, Douglas Fairbanks was honored by the University of Southern California Fencing Club for his involvement in fencing which became one of his silent and talking film signatures. He often played swashbuckling roles as in *Robin Hood*, *The Thief of Bagdad*, *The Mark of Zorro*, *The Private Life of Don Juan*, *Black Pirate*, and *The Gaucho*. All in all, Douglas Fairbanks acted, wrote, produced, and/or directed 51 films.

Fairbanks and Pickford played opposite one another in Shakespeare's *The Taming of the Shrew*. In 1916, Douglas Fairbanks appeared in a dark comedy, *The Mystery of the Leaping Frog*, about cocaine use.

Douglas and Mary Fairbanks and their friend Charlie Chaplin sold war bonds during the First World War after Fairbank's was rejected for service because of varicose veins. The Fairbank's put their hands in wet concrete in front of Grumman's Chinese Theatre thereby starting the Hollywood Walk of Fame.

Mary Pickford, born Gladys Louise Smith, began acting at age 7 and was called the 24th greatest female actor of all time; she appeared in 52 feature films and an astounding 51 films during one year, including short films for the war effort. One of her earliest stage appearances was as Little Eva in *Uncle Tom's Cabin*.

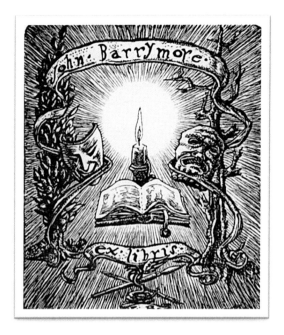

At the insistence of David Belasco, Gladys changed her name to the stage name of Mary Pickford. During her marriage to Douglas Fairbanks, they built a home called Pickfair, which she retained after their divorce. Pickfair became the center of Hollywood life, its guests including Charlie Chaplin, George Bernard Shaw, Albert Einstein, Helen Keller, H. G. Wells, Lord Louis Mountbatten, Fritz Kreisler, Amelia Earhart, F. Scott Fitzgerald, Noel Coward and Arthur Conant Doyle, and dozens of other famous persons.

John Barrymore
Engraver Unknown
(Plate 21015)

If ever there was an American theater family, it would be that of the Barrymore's. **John Barrymore** aka **John Sydney Blyth** (1882—1942) was the son, father and grandfather of actors. He was the brother of Ethel and Lionel Barrymore, the father of John Drew Barrymore, and the grandfather of actress Drew Barrymore. The son, John Drew Barrymore, is Drew Barrymore's father. He acted in 34 major film and television dramas, but had a career impoverished by drugs and alcohol. His daughter is still active in the film and television industry.

John Barrymore Sr. began his career with light comedy, but soon became a Shakespearean star playing Hamlet and Richard III. He appeared in silent and sound films, and established a record on Broadway as Hamlet in 101 performances.

Although many of his relatives have received Hollywood awards, John Sr. only received one which he gave to himself. He has a star on the Hollywood walk of fame. John Barrymore Sr. had 4 wives and 3 children. Three of his wives were actresses and one a poet.

David Belasco
Engraver Unknown
(Plate 21016)

David Belasco (1853—1931) was born in San Francisco because his parents, Sephardic Jews, immigrated to California for the 1849 Gold Rush. Their son started in the theatre as a script copier and call boy, but showed a talent for learning and doing just about everything in show business, eventually rising to become one of the most successful producer-directors ever on the New York stage where he wrote, directed, produced and/or acted in more than 100 Broadway plays. During his life, he built two

Broadway theaters, and several more were constructed in other cities.

Belasco adapted a short story called "Madame Butterfly" into a play, and wrote another called *The Girl of the Golden West*. Both became subjects for operas by Giacomo Puccini and have become subjects for numerous other productions. More than 40 motion pictures have been made from Belasco's plays and scripts.

Actors and film makers sought out opportunities to work with David Belasco, including Cecil B. DeMille, D.W. Griffith, Helen Hayes, Lillian Gish, Mary Pickford, and Lionel and Maurice Barrymore. Belasco's contributions to the American stage were huge; he is credited with bringing naturalism into theatre productions and with utilizing the latest mechanical and scientific advances in his productions.

Jean Hersholt
Engraver Jean Hersholt
(Plate 21012)

Jean Hersholt (1886—1956) was a Danish born actor who worked in radio, television, and films. He played Shirley Temple's grandfather in Heidi, and his credits include 75 silent films and 65 sound films, four of which he directed. Hersholt's parents were actors in the Danish Folk Theatre. He was Dr. Christian in a radio series directed by Neil Reagan, the brother of actor Ronald Reagan. Jean Hersholt was awarded two honorary academy awards for his service to the industry, and has the Jean Hersholt Humanitarian Award named after him.

Jean Hersholt loved Hans Christian Anderson and translated over 140 of his stories into the English language. His translations are still recognized as among the best renditions of Andersen's stories. Hersholt designed his own bookplate, titled "Knowledge is Power."

William Charles Macready
Engraver Unknown
(Plate 21033)

William Charles Macready (1793—1873) was a highly regarded theater manager and actor, as was his father. The son played at Covent Garden, Drury Lane Theatre, and

100

toured in Paris and New York. At Drury Lane, he managed and performed lead roles in *Henry V* by Shakespeare, *The Two Foscaris* by Byron, *Strafford* by Robert Browning, and *The Lady of Lyons and Richelieu* by Bulwar-Lytton. He also acted in *Macbeth*, *King Lear*, and *Hamlet*. Macready was known for bringing historical authenticity to his productions, and was among the first to refer back to Shakespeare's originals for scripts.

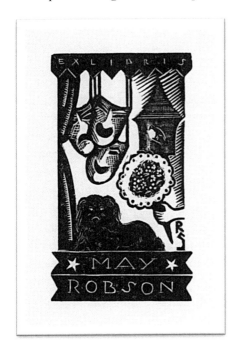

May Robson
Engraver Ruth Thompson Saunders
(Plate 21010)

An Australian by birth, **May Robson** (1858—1942) was one of the most prolific of performing artists to come to Hollywood during its early years. She acted in 60 films of which 8 were silent and 52 were sound movies. She was most known for her portrayals of a cranky old lady who has a golden heart in the end. Robson was the earliest-born person to be nominated for an Academy Award at age 75; Katherine Hepburn won that year. She appeared in *Red Headed Woman* (1932), *Anna Karenina* (1935), *A Star is Born* (1937) and *Joan of Paris* (1942).

May Robson's bookplate (1933) is by **Ruth Thompson Saunders**, an Australian bookplate engraver who worked in wood.

Otis Skinner
Engraver Edith Emerson
(Plate 21002)

The father of Cornelia Otis Skinner, **Otis Skinner** (1858—1942) excelled in Shakespearean roles such as Shylock, Hamlet, Richard III and Romeo, employing a naturalistic acting style. He became a leading man after working in the company of Edwin Booth and Helena Modjeska. Other roles included Sancho Panza and Falstaff.

EX LIBRIS

Walt Disney
Engraver Unknown
(Plate 21006)

Now the most recognized person in Hollywood history, **Walt Disney** (1901—1966) achieved phenomenal success as a businessman after starting the Walt Disney Company with his brother, Roy. Together they built the Company into one of the largest film production units in Hollywood, and pioneered dozens of innovations, particularly those related to animation. Later in life, the Disney Corporation created theme parks in California and Florida as well as in Tokyo, Paris and Hong Kong that are tourist destinations to this day.

During his career, Walt Disney was awarded 4 honorary Academy Awards, won another 22 himself, and received 7 Emmys. Disney has two stars in the Hollywood Walk of Fame. He worked as an animator, producer, director, screenwriter, voice actor, and philanthropist.

Just after the World War I, he drove an ambulance for the Red Cross in France. Disney began drawing pictures before high school, and attended art school where he learned how to draw cartoons for newspapers. He and his brother set up their first studio in Hollywood in 1923, and developed the cartoon characters of Mickey Mouse, Goofy, Donald Duck, Snow White and the Seven Dwarfs, and dozens of other cartoon character icons. Disney Studios began producing films including Alice in Wonderland and Peter Pan which were finished after World War II. His theme parks were begun in the 1950s.

Walt Disney's ancestry stems from one Robert d'Isigny who traveled with William the Conqueror to England in 1066. The spelling d'Isigny became Disney in later generations.

Among the less attractive aspects of Walt Disney's life was his participation in the Red Scare of the 1950s where he became a favorite of the FBI by personally labelling several Hollywood professionals as members of the Communist Party, unproven accusations that ruined their careers and subjected several to governmental harassment and worse.

Charles Chaplin
Engraver Unknown
(Plate 21008)

Sir Charles Spencer "Charlie" Chaplin (1889—1977) was a comedian, actor and filmmaker who, according to his biographers, participated in every aspect of his films. Early in his career he co-founded, with his friends Douglas Fairbanks and Mary Pickford, United Artists which gave each of them total control over their films and careers. Chaplin wrote, directed, produced, edited, starred in, and composed music for his movies. Among the most known of his films are *The Gold Rush, City Lights, Modern Times* and *The Great Dictator* which industry surveys often rank as the greatest films of all time.

Charlie Chaplin entered the film industry during the silent era and refused to move into sound in the 1930s even as the industry was embracing it. His first film was titled *Making a Living* by Keystone Productions in 1914, and by 1918 he was among the best known figures in the world, largely because of his compelling portrayals as the tramp in his movies. He did *The Kid* (1921), *A Woman of Paris* (1923), *The Gold Rush* (1925) and *The Circus* (1928).

The Great Dictator (1940) satirized Adolph Hitler and exposed Chaplin to the ire of the radical right in America. The 'right' was led by J. Edgar Hoover's FBI and the House of Un-American Activities Committee who were determined to find communists under every director's chair. Focusing on a

paternity suit brought by a former mistress of Chaplin's, the FBI investigated Chaplin with a vengeance and eventually caused him to move to Switzerland. He stayed away from America for the next 20 years, meanwhile creating some of the most important and artistic films in the industry.

Charles Chaplin's third wife was Oona O'Neill, daughter of American playwright Eugene O'Neill, with whom he had eight children.

James Cagney
Engraver Unknown
(Plate 21011)

A successful and convincing "tough guy" of the movies, **James Cagney** (1899—1986), began as a comic and vaudeville tap dancer on Broadway for 10 years. His breakthrough film was *The Public Enemy* (1931) which became the most influential of gangster movies. He followed it with *Taxi* in 1931 in which he shoved a

103

grapefruit into the face of his female co-star, *Angels with Dirty Faces* (1938), and *White Heat* (1949). He received an Oscar for playing George M. Cohen in *Yankee Doodle Dandy* in which he also danced on screen. The famous line, "You dirty rat!" was never said by Cagney, but he did say "Come out and take it! You yellow-bellied rat!" in one of his movies.

James Cagney has been ranked 8th among the 50 greatest screen legends, and Orson Welles said Cagney was "maybe the greatest actor who ever appeared in front of a camera." His first movie was *Sinner's Holiday* (1930), *Frisco Kid* (1935), *The Strawberry Blonde* (1941), *and Mister Roberts* (1955). His last film was *Ragtime* (1961). During his career, James Cagney made 66 movies.

Cagney had been an amateur boxer in his younger life, and one time was a runner up for the New York state amateur lightweight boxing title. He also played semi-professional baseball, and later in life pursued interests in farming, horses, sailing, and he owned two working farms.

Cagney was accused of being a communist sympathizer in 1934 and again in 1940 as part of the Hollywood Red Scare and J. Edgar Hoover's paranoiac pursuit of shadows but although it caused Cagney considerable stress little came of it.

Chapter VII: Writers, Artists and Illustrators

As early as Rembrandt bookplate engraving combined line engraving with etching. The early British engravers used armorial and heraldic motifs to characterize their plates and to provide owner identification. Much of the British style of engraving was employed in early American bookplate engraving even though citizens of the new country did not have a history of monarchies nor a class privileged by birthright to be embodied in the designs of their bookplates.

Designers and engravers, often at the insistence of bookplate owners, either harkened back to the English traditions of design or developed new motifs for their plates. In both cases, the new Americans (and Australians) demonstrated skill and artistic talent equal to their "old world" predecessors. One purchaser of a bookplate, M.C.D Borden, requested that the British crown engraved by E. B. Bird on a proof copy of his bookplate be changed to an American eagle to better represent Borden's U.S. nationality.

An interesting aspect of the development of the art of bookplate design in the late 18th century is its close relationship to historical events. The American and French Revolutions brought new forms of government—democratically based—to the western world. Observers and historians began to include motifs of these events in their work. The Boston Tea Party and the Concord Massacre became subjects for Paul Revere who himself had an active role in the American Revolution.

Early designs imitated the British designs without the heraldic provenance. Relatively speaking, bookplates were expensive acquisitions, thus their owners came from wealthy or privileged classes. With the invention of photo engraving and more recently digital technology, engraving of bookplates by hand became less of an art and more a technological creation. Some modern artists, however, continue to accept commissions for bookplates.

Lafayette's bookplate includes symbols of his French lineage and seafaring occupation. Alexander Hamilton's plate has the tree of life and sailing ships among its motifs. Symbolization of personal history and culture through design characteristics occurs throughout the history of bookplate engraving. Modern bookplate designs often are characteristic of late 20th and 21st century themes and events.

Historians of bookplate engraving point out that its development traversed through several stages and systems of classification. **John Byrne Leicester Warren** (later known as Baron de Tabley) came up with the following classification in 1880:

> Early Armorial, 1500—1700 heraldry and the family crest;
> Jacobean Style, 1700—1740 stiff and heavy;
> Chippendale, or rococo, 1740—1775 shields with scrolls and shell work;
> The Ribbon and Wreath, or Festoon, 1775—1780 decorative chain or script;
> Modern Armorial, 1800—1880 family crest, but with names.

Warren's classification was expanded by **Charles Dexter Allen (**1865—1926):

> Allegorical, with scenes from art or history;
> Landscape, depicting a favorite view;
> Portraits, often used in memorial plates in libraries;
> Literary, showing a shelf of books or library corners;
> Rebus, punning or canting plate especially popular with the French.

American engravers followed the French by including humor in their designs, as is amply shown in the plates that follow. Another greatly expanded 33 item classification system was provided by **Zella Allen Dixson** in her *Concerning Bookplates: a handbook for Collectors* (1903). Her book is available on line through Project Gutenberg. She delineates the earlier categories and adds a section on French bookplates. In the end, however, she says the most efficient system for categorizing bookplates may be alphabetical within country.

There are two categories of plates that are not expressly indicated by the Warren-Allen-Dixson classification systems. Included in many plates are the occupations or occupational heritages of the plate owners, particularly those in exploration and seafaring. Another theme that frequently appears in modern bookplates is a nude or erotic motif, several examples of which appear in this chapter.

Clara Tice "Bruno's Garret"
Engraver Clara Tice
(Plate 33062)

Although **Clara Tice** (1888—1973) was not the earliest or the most important artist in the history of bookplates, her etchings have simplicity and visual allure that made her both famous and infamous.

In 1915, a small pamphlet was published called *Bruno's Garret* that featured several of Clara Tice's etchings. The line drawings in these etchings generally portrayed young nude women in nature (mountains, butterflies, peacocks). Her designs are tame by today's standards, but in 1915—the end of the Victorian era and the beginning of the "roaring 20s"—pictures such as these were avant-garde and stimulated religious protests against their appearing in public.

Tice's drawings communicate an innocence and freedom that disappeared with the Great Depression. Her designs are often released today as large posters, and her original work is highly prized by collectors.

Clara Tice "Two Girls with Peacock"\
Engraver Clara Tice\
(Plate 33054)

Clara Tice came to fame in 1915 because a retired captain of the Society for the Suppression of Vice in New York decided her work was too provocative for public display and raided an exhibition of her work in Greenwich Village. Headlines in the New York papers and a mock trial at Bruno's Garret conducted by the editor of *Vanity Fair* for whom Tice worked became a public defense in which "the charges of having committed unspeakable, black atrocities on white paper, abusing slender bodies of girls, cats, peacocks and butterflies" were debunked.

Clara Tice "Three Girls in a Fountain"\
Engraver Clara Tice\
(Plate 33057)

Bruno's Weekly Gallery was a magazine published in the New York Greenwich Village area by Charles Edison, son of Thomas Edison, and edited by Guido Bruno at his garret in Washington Square, NYC. The *Weekly* printed many modern artists and writers work, including the etchings of Clara Tice. She was acquainted with Marcel Duchamp whose "Nude Descending a Staircase" now located at the Philadelphia Museum of Art was exhibited in the *Exhibition du arte Cubist* in 1912.

Even though she did a few bookplates, Clara Tice's primary work was in painting, larger etchings and illustrating. One of several books she provided drawings for was *Aphrodite* by Pierre Louys in 1926; only limited edition copies were printed, and now the book is a collector's prize.

Vicente Blasco Ibanez (1867—1928) was a Spanish writer of several books, one called *Los cuatro jinetes del Apocalipsis* 1916 or *The Four Horsemen of the Apocalypse*. It is about two brothers-in-law fighting on opposite sides during the World War I. A movie of this book gave fame and stardom to Rudolph Valentino. Several of Ibanez's books have been made into movies. Ibanez was noted for his writing realism. Among Ibanez's interests were politics and women. He is said to have had several stormy love affairs, and was almost killed when a bullet lodged itself in a belt buckle.

Vicente Blasco Ibanez
Engraver Senor Ismael Smith (Plate 23056 a d)

 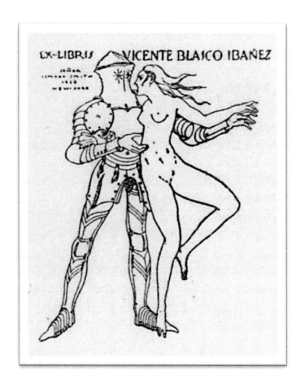

Ibanez's bookplates were executed by **Senor Ismael Smith (**1886—1972) and were exhibited in 1921 at the Sixth Annual Exhibition of the American Bookplate Society (later to become the American Society of Bookplate Collectors and Designers). Smith's designs are highly collectable and held in several libraries and museums. Smith's line drawings are similar to Tice's etchings both in style and content.

Georges de Hemptinne
Engraver Harold E. Nelson
(Plate 41076)

Harold Edward Hughes Nelson (1871—1948) was a designer of bookplates and illustrator of books who worked in the art deco style. One of his works was *St. George and the Dragon*, a postage stamp design he produced for the 1929 Postal Union Conference.

Nelson was born in Dorchester, England, but lived in London most of his life. His first bookplate appeared in 1897, inspired by Albrecht Durer. The Nelson plate for Georges de Hemptinne has an interesting French motif design but there is little other available information about the plate or de Hemptinne.

John Lumsden Property
Engraver Aubrey Beardsley
(Plate 09002)

Aubrey Beardsley (1872—1898) just designed three bookplates himself but his pen and ink illustrations have been used by others to create several dozen bookplates in his style. One of Oscar Taylor Blackburn's bookplates was reminiscent of the style of Aubrey Beardsley.

Aubrey Beardsley lived only 25 years, but his images are known worldwide. He was part of the aesthetic or Art Nouveau (new art) movement that was identified with Oscar Wilde and James A. McNeill Whistler. Beardsley did illustrations for Wilde's play *Salome* as well as other literary works like Aristophanes' *Lysistrata* that emphasized the 'decadent, grotesque and erotic', a disposition for which Oscar Wilde went to prison.

Beardsley was said to be influenced by the Japanese woodblock prints that came into Europe during the 19th century as wrapping paper around porcelains imported from Japan, as well as by Henri de Toulouse-Lautrec's poster art.

A copy of Beardsley's "Clown on a Stage" recently sold for 117 pounds.

Franz von Bayros (1866—1924) was an Austrian commercial artist and illustrator who belonged to the art Decadent Movement of the early 20th century of which Aubrey Beardsley was a member. von Bayros was born in Zagreb of the Austrian Empire, now Croatia. Although he created over 2,000 drawings during his lifetime, von Bayros' work was banned in a succession of European capitals as being too outrageous.

Paul Himmelreich
Engraver Franz von Bayros
(Plate 19011)

Besides bookplates, von Bayros drew images for books such as *The Divine Comedy* by Dante. Although his nude pictures are explicit, by today's standards they are not as outrageous as they once were, and his work can be found in major American and European museums.

Leda and the Swan
Engraver Franz von
Bayros
(Plate 19040)

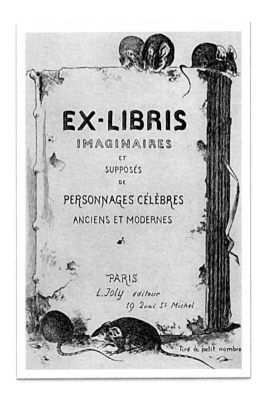

L. Joly
"Ex Libris Imaginaires
et Supposes de Personnages
Celebres Anciens et Modernes"
(Plate 37002)

A French publisher named **L. Joly** (cir. 1895) issued a series of 35 bookplates as they might have looked for ancient and modern celebrities. Among the designs were plates for Edgar Allen Poe, French General Marat, the Marquis de Sade and the writer Baudelaire.

De A DAM
William Fowler Hopson
(Plate 37003)

The Blackburn Collection has about 50 **William Fowler Hopson** (1849—1935) bookplate engravings, many of them signed, including the humorous bookplate for A DAM that he did for the Joly *Imaginaire* publication.

Victor Hugo
Engraver Joly/Unknown
(Plate 37024)

Of all French writers, **Victor Hugo** (1802—1885) is probably the most respected and best known. Every major city in France has a street or park named after him, and he has been celebrated in music, art, music and literature innumerable times.

The imaginary Victor Hugo plate from Joly's publication shows a frog seated next to a cliff looking at the sea with Hugo's name in a sunburst. Hugo's other bookplate, one commissioned or designed by him, shows a broken cathedral with VH, Hugo's initials, superimposed in front of it.

It is said that Hugo's characterizations of the Cathedral of Notre Dame in his *The Hunchback of Notre Dame* resulted in shaming the French government into providing funds for its restoration.

Victor Hugo wrote poetry, plays, novels and essays, and produced 4,000 drawings during his life, and is said to have foreshadowed surrealism and abstract expressionism. Over 100 operas have been based on Hugo's works, and several films and musical scores have been written, most recently *Les Miserables* by Andrew Lloyd Webber.

He also was a human rights campaigner who was instrumental in abolishing the death penalty in Geneva, Portugal and Columbia. He argued for clemency for Maximillian, Emperor of Mexico and John Brown, both to no avail. Among his books was *The Last Day of a Condemned Man*, his first written against the guillotine that is said to have influenced Albert Camus, *Reflections on a Guillotine*. Another of Hugo's books was *The End of Satan and God* in which he characterized Christianity as a griffin and Rationalism as an angel.

Although Hugo initially supported Napoleon, he called Napoleon III a traitor to France, and chose to live in exile for fifteen years on the island of Guernsey until the fall of Napoleon III. Two of Hugo's friends were Berlioz and Franz Liszt who once played Beethoven for Hugo.

The French engraver of Hugo's 1870 bookplate was Aglaus Bouvenne. Bouvenne was an artist and writer who wrote several books about artists and ex libris. Among his ex libris plates were one for Theophile Gautier and another for Madame Noe whose husband also was a noted artist of the time.

François Rabelais
Engraver Joly/Unknown
(Plate 37028)

Francois Rabelais (1483—1553) was a French writer, doctor, humanist, monk and Greek scholar. He wrote fantasy, satire, humor, grotesque bawdy jokes, and songs. As a Greek scholar and physician, he translated Hippocrates and Galen. Rabelais is considered one of the great writers in world literature.

His most famous book, *Gargantua and Pantagruel* satirized almost everything, but especially the Catholic Church. Rabelais in his younger years was a novice in the Franciscan order and a friar at Fontenay le Comte, and at the Benedictine order at Maillezines. One of his more memorable phrases about a character was "he was the best monk that ever monked the monkery." *Gargantua and Pantagruel* takes place at the imaginary Abby of Theleme, a place without clocks, a swimming pool for the monks, and staffed with maids who provided services.

The last words Rabelais is said to have spoken on his death bed were "I go to seek the Great Perhaps."

Alexandre Dumas
Engraver Joly/Unknown
(Plate 37033)

The theme of the imaginary plate for **Alexandre Dumas** (1802—1870) is based on his book, *The Great Dictionary of Cuisine* and the 38 novels he wrote in his lifetime, plus several plays, magazine articles, and travel books. Said to have written over 100,000 pages, his works have been translated into over 100 languages and are the subject of numerous movies and musical pieces. Three of his novels are *The Count of Monte Cristo*, *The Three Musketeers*, and *The Vicomte de Bragelonne: Ten Years Later*.

Alexandre Dumas was born Dumas Davy de la Pailletrie. His grandfather was a military member of the French aristocracy, and his grandmother was a former slave of Afro-Caribbean ancestry. Once a man insulted Dumas' ancestry; Dumas said, "My father was a mulatto, my grandfather was a Negro, and my great-grandfather was a monkey. You see, Sir, my family starts where yours ends." Dumas had several 'natural' children, and supposedly had as many as 40 affairs with women, one being the American actress Adah Isaacs Menken, who at the time was at the top of her career. One son, also named Alexandre Dumas, was a writer of novels and plays.

Miguel de Cervantes (1547—1616) died within a day (or 10 days given the difference of the Georgian and Julian calendars) of William Shakespeare. Cervantes was a novelist, poet, playwright, soldier and for five years a slave who created two of the most known characters in literature, Don Quixote and Sancho Panza.

Miguel de Cervantes
Engraver Joly/Unknown
(Plate 37034)

Besides the novel *Don Quixote*, Cervantes wrote *Novelas Ejemplares* which consists of 12 short stories, *Los Trabajos de Persiles y Sigismunda*, *Viaje del Parnoso*, and *La Numancia*. It is said that his influence on the Spanish language is so great that it is often called la lengua de Cervantes. While a soldier in the Spanish Navy Marines, he received 3 gunshot wounds in the battle of Lepanto that left on arm paralyzed for a time. Later on his return trip, his boat was attacked and he ended up a prisoner in Algiers for five years but was eventually ransomed after four failed escape attempts.

Louis-Napoleon Bonaparte
Engraver Joly/Unknown
(Plate 37014)

The imaginary bookplate for **Louis-Napoleon Bonaparte** (1769—1821) shows a book with the word "Code", a reference to the Napoleonic Code or legal code that forbade privilege based on birth, guaranteed religious freedom, and influenced civil law worldwide.

Once Napoleon became the Emperor of France, he engaged in several Napoleonic Wars that initiated the French Revolution. Napoleon's campaigns resulted in the French conquest of most of Europe, but ended in a disastrous winter in Russia and after exile and return to power at Waterloo, where he was defeated by Wellington. Napoleon's military tactics are still studied in war colleges around the world.

Napoleon married twice. His first wife was Josephine de Beauharnais, a widow of the Reign of Terror in the French revolution. While he was off conquering the world, they both had affairs, and their marriage ended in divorce. He then married the Archduchess of Austria who was a great grandniece of Marie Antoinette; he remained married to her until his death. She did not follow him into exile either on the isle of Alba or St. Helena, where Bonaparte spent the last six years of his life. Napoleon Bonaparte had several illegitimate children. One of Bonaparte's sons, Napoleon II, was Emperor for two weeks until he died of tuberculosis.

Francois Boucher
Engraver Joly/Unknown
(Plate 37018)

Francois Boucher (1703—1770) was a French painter in the Rococo style, which had a lot of curves, witty themes, and flourishes. Many of the heraldic bookplates include aspects of rococo style in them. Boucher used classical themes with nudes in many of his paintings, and also painted (in full dress) his patroness, Madame de Pompadour who was a mistress of King Louis V.

De Musset
Engraver Joly/Unknown
(Plate 37029)

An early writer of romanticism, **Alfred de Musset** (1810—1857) wrote *The Confession of a Child of the Century*, an autobiographical novel about his love affair with George Sand. As shown in the imaginary bookplate, de Musset's *Confession* tells of Sand's lesbian leanings together with his own participation..

Bouquinistes are used book sellers who since the 1500s have been located along the Seine around Notre-Dame in Paris. During the French revolution, many of the grand estates libraries were liberated to be sold by the bouquinistes.

The engraver, **Joseph Apoux** (cir. 1880--1910) is largely unknown but famous for the creation of an erotic alphabet—a series of pornographic pictures set on the shapes of the alphabet. L. Joly published a set of engravings by Joseph Apoux called "Six Caprices"; Apoux also designed a few bookplates, including one for Danton in this series but not included here.

Maxim Gorky (1868—1936) was a Russian novelist and playwright as well as a political activist associated with the Marxist socialist democratic movement. As a young man, Gorky was orphaned and raised by his grandmother. He tried to commit suicide once, and traveled across the Russian empire on foot for five years.

Among Gorky's acquaintances and friends were political activists Vladimir Lenin, Joseph Stalin, and Vyacheslav Molotov, and writers Anton Chekhov and Leo Tolstoy. Born Nizhny Novgorod, he assumed the name pen name 'Gorky' which means 'bitter'.

Although Gorky rose to fame during the time of Tsar Nicholas II, his political writing and activism caused him to be imprisoned several times. After "Bloody Sunday" that began the 1905 Revolution, he spent time in and out of exile. The Socialist

117

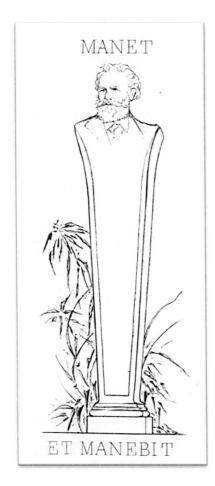

MANET

ET MANEBIT

government sent him to the United States to raise money, where he wrote a novel called *The Mother*—later adapted to a play by Berthold Brecht—and caused a scandal because he traveled with his mistress rather than his wife. Gorky's most famous play, *The Lower Depths*, describes people on the margins and in the lowest strata of society. Both Lenin and Molotov were pallbearers at Gorky's funeral, but Gorky may have been killed by the Russian government, glad to be rid of an uncontrollable political nuisance.

Edouart Manet
Engraver Unknown
(Plate 12020)

The French painter, **Edouart Manet** (1832—1883) studied the old masters by painting copies of their works at the Louvre and was friends with several of the most prominent painters of his day including Edgar Degas, Claud Monet, Pierre August Renoir, Alfred Sisley, Paul Cezanne, Berthe Morisot, and Camille Pissarro.

Manet is regarded as a pivotal figure in the transition from realism to impressionism. Three of his paintings were titled "Luncheon on the Grass" (1863), "Olympia" (1863), and "A Bar at the Follies Bergere" (1882). His use of nude female models together with clothed male models provided enough controversy that his painting was rejected by the Paris Salon; he later exhibited it in the Salon de Refuses.

"Olympia" reveals a nude woman with a clothed woman in the background in a pose on a couch similar to Goya's "Naked Maja". The line drawing of the woman shows the influence of the Japanese wood block prints that were entering France about this time.

Many of Manet's later paintings were of people in ordinary settings—"The Railway", "The Spanish Singer", "The Dead Matador" for example, focus on the individuals with little emphasis on background. Manet also did three large paintings of "The Execution of Emperor Maximillian".

Joseph Mallard William Turner (1775—1851) was an English Romantic landscape painter and printmaker who is also credited as being a master of British watercolor landscape painting. Many of his paintings are bright, sunlit vistas or buildings, but his first and many to follow was an oil painting called "The Fisherman" that was a fisherman's boat set on a dark sea at night illuminated by the moon through storm clouds. The Romantic style of Turner was indicated by his use of natural phenomena such as sunlight, storms, rain and fog.

Turner's personal life was dedicated to art. He had a relationship with a widowed woman and may have been the father of two of her children, and when he died, it was at the home of his mistress, Sophia Caroline Booth. His exact birth date is unverified, but Turner claimed he was born of St. George's Day, April 23, which happens to be the day William Shakespeare was born in 1564 and the day both he and Cervantes died in 1616.

Besides designing his own bookplate that is said to be extremely rare, **Frederic Remington** (1861—1909) designed at least two other bookplates, one for Alfred Henry Lewis and another for Louis Winchester Jones. Each of these bookplates embodies a cowboy or western motif that was the signature theme of all of Remington's works.

Frederick Remington was the cousin of Eliphalet Remington, the founder of the Remington Arms Company, the oldest firearms company in America. Frederick Remington was an American artist, writer, painter, illustrator, and sculptor whose realistic images of cowboys and American Indians helped define the American west. Frederick Remington was distantly related to George Catlin (painter of American Indians) and Earl Bascom (American printmaker, sculptor, rodeo performer), and his father was a colonel in the American Civil War.

One of Remington's credits is he is the first American artist to represent the true gait of a horse in motion, and he invented the idea of the "cowboy sculpture" that still appears in Western art. He did 83 illustrations for a book by Theodore Roosevelt called *Ranch Life and the Hunting Trail*, and used sand casting and lost wax method for his classic sculptures.

Ozias Humphrey
Engraver Unknown
(Plate 12035)

An English portrait painter of miniatures, **Ozias Humphry** (1742—1810) was appointed Portrait Painter to the King in Crayons (pastels) and did several paintings of royalty. He had been encouraged to study painting by Thomas Gainsborough, himself a painter of portraits and landscapes.

Because of failing eyesight and unfortunately ending up blind, Humphry painted larger and larger pieces. Many of his pictures are of Asian scenes where he traveled in India during the Raj for several years. Among his portraits were Joseph Priestly and Jane Austin.

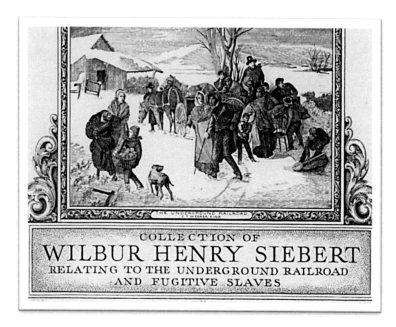

Wilbur Henry Siebert "Underground Railroad"
Engraver A.N. MacDonald
(Plate 32039)

Wilbur Henry Siebert (1866—1961) was a Harvard educated historian who wrote *The Underground Railroad from Slavery to Freedom* published in 1898. Siebert assembled a large collection of Underground Railroad materials, many of which are still being substantiated by more recent researchers. His bookplate was engraved by **A. N. (Arthur Nelson) MacDonald** in 1935.

Eli Whitney
Engraver W. F. Hopson
(Plate 02021)

Best known for his invention of the cotton gin, which has been called one of the key inventions of the Industrial Revolution, **Eli Whitney** (1765—1825) also advocated the concept of 'interchangeable parts'.

'Interchangeable parts' was an idea Whitney got from Europe; he used it to win a contract for manufacturing muskets for the U.S. Army. Although he didn't know anything about gun manufacturing, he had worked with his father during the American Revolutionary War in the manufacture of iron nails. The use of interchangeable parts in rifles helped the North win the Civil War.

W. F. Hopson (1849—1935), the engraver of Eli Whitney's bookplate, was a painter, engraver, etcher, and book illustrator. He is most known for his bookplates. As a professional engraver, Hopson did over 2,000 small illustrative engraved pictures for *Webster's Unabridged Dictionary*, and in another book created a large number of pictures of extinct North American animals. In 1900, W. F. Hopson exhibited at the 1900 Paris Exposition. He was a member of the Grolier Society, and the Club of Odd Volumes.

John and Ethel Van Derlip
Engraver Maxfield Parrish
(Plate 30009)

Maxfield Parrish (1870—1960) produced over 900 paintings, illustrations and bookplates. His influence, however, continues to this day, and he was one of 18 artists featured on the U.S. Artists Stamp series, along with Rockwell Kent, Norman Rockwell, Frederic Remington and others. One of his series of illustrations was for *The Thousand and One Arabian Nights* edited by Kate Douglas Wiggin and Nora A Smith which can be obtained through Project Gutenberg. Norman Rockwell called Parrish "my idol". All of Parrish's work is highly collectible, and his paintings sell for high prices.

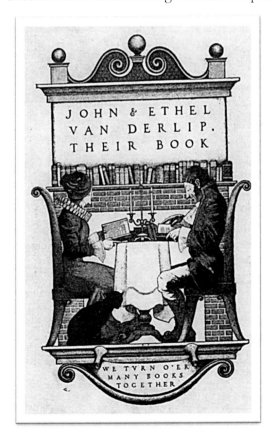

H. S. Marks
Engraver H.S. Marks
(Plate 12025)

Henry Stacy Marks (1829—1898) was an English painter who painted Shakespearean themes and themes from classical sculpture and literature. He is featured in the Victoria and Albert Museum and has works hung in American museums as well. Three of his titles are The Franciscan Sculptor and His Model (1860) for which he received 300 pounds, The Atheist and the Acorn (1863) and An Odd Volume (1894) that shows a book collector reading an old volume. Marks spent time studying in Paris, and painted on glass for a commercial company during his early career.

W. Bradley
Engraver Adrian Feint
(Plate 12024)

Recent examples of woodcuts are the plates created by **Adrian Feint** (1894—1971), an Australian engraver working in the 1930s. Feint autographed his bookplates for inclusion in the *Yearbook of the American Society of Bookplate Collectors and Designers.*

Feint began his career creating decorative pen and ink drawings and illustrations but became famous for his woodcuts and book plates. He joined with Perce Green to publish Tench's Narrative of an Expedition to Botany Bay which is the story of 212 officers and marines who in 1788 brought 760 convicts to settle in Australia at the penal colony where Sydney is now located.

Mary Wilson Blackwood
Engraver Adrian Feint
(Plate 31043)

John Bertram Norris
Engraver Adrian Feint
(Plate 31048)

Feint turned, in his later career, to painting and has become one of Australia's most important artists. His engravings and paintings are highly collectable.

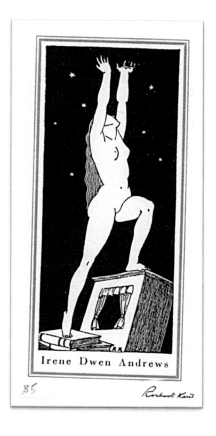

Rockwell Kent (1882—1971) produced dozens of woodcut bookplates and marks, and illustrated several literary works including a very highly prized 3 volume set of *Moby Dick*. He created several bookplates for **Irene Dwen Andrews** in the Art Deco style prevalent in the 1920's.

Andrews was a book and bookplate collector, as well as a printer, who commissioned many bookplates for herself from most of the bookplate artists of her day. Irene Dwen Andrews's bookplate collection, said to be 250,000 plates, is housed at Yale University.

Leroy Truman Goble
Engraver Ralph Pearson
(Plate 39006)

An American etcher, **Ralph M. Pearson** (1883—1958), working in New Mexico during the 1920s produced a much softer landscape and figure scene for Leroy Truman Goble. Pearson's etchings are highly sought after by art and bookplate collectors.

Chapter VIII: Bookplate Designers and Engravers

The Blackburn Collection contains over 3,200 bookplates designed and/or engraved by dozens of bookplate artists who lived and worked during four centuries.

Most of the bookplates selected for this book were engraved by artists living in England, the United States, Germany, France and Australia. The history of bookplate engraving, however, reveals the earliest engravers likely were from China and Japan. More recently, engravers have lived on the African continent, in other countries of Europe and Russia, and in Central Asian countries. More than a few bookplate artists are from Central America, particularly Mexico.

Motifs, themes and styles of engraving often reflected the origins of the bookplates, and occasionally historical influences across cultures. For example, in Beardsley's drawings one can see the influence of Japanese woodblock prints. American plates are often reminiscent of English ancestors, such as shown in George Washington's bookplate.

This chapter focuses on a few bookplate designers and engravers not featured in earlier chapters. They were chosen based on indications of their importance in the bookplate literature of the time—articles written for the *American Society of Bookplate Collectors and Designers Yearbooks*, and books about engraving and collecting written during the period covered by the Blackburn Collection.

Elisha Brown Bird
Engraver Elisha Brown Bird
(Plate 01028)

Elisha Brown Bird (1867—1943) trained for four years at the Massachusetts Institute of Technology in architecture, design, decorative figure work and lettering. Although he began his career in commercial art, his first bookplate was engraved in 1892 and by 1910 he focused on bookplate design and engraving for a career. Bird spent over 50 years creating more than 200 bookplates. His plates have been categorized as those created on zinc, those done through a photogravure etching process, and those that were designs to be hand engraved on copper.

Carlyle S. Baer, writing about bookplate and engraving design, points out that Bird's designs have been engraved by the three greatest bookplate engravers of the 20th century—Edwin Davis French, J. Winfred Spenceley, and Sidney L. Smith. Baer also characterized Bird as equally skilled in drawing human figures, heraldry, nature motifs, and angling scenes. "His plates for women are peculiarly feminine, both in design and execution" said Baer.

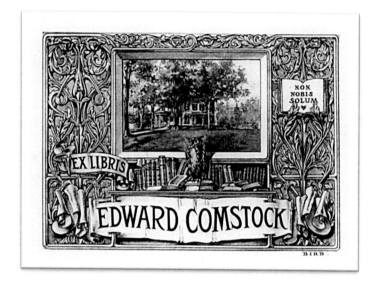

Edward Comstock
Engraver Elisha Brown Bird 1867—1943
(Plate 01019)

As shown in the Comstock plate, Bird's engravings are highly ornate, and in this case infused with nature, architectural, library and classic motifs. "Non Noblis Solum" is a Latin phrase meaning "not for ourselves alone".

Wikipedia reports this saying was derived from Cicero's translation of Plato and generally is taken to mean that humans have been created for the sake of others of their kind, not for themselves alone.

William Fowler Hopson (1849—1935) was often referred to as America's leading cutter in wood, although he was said to be equally comfortable engraving on wood and copper and producing etchings. Between 1892 and 1910 he had created 102 bookplates with library, literary, pictorial, and architectural motifs. Charles Dexter Allen said "Hopson has a fondness for the out of doors, a sense of the humorous, loyalty to friends, and an unfailing sense of the artistic" all of which show up in his bookplates.

Tobias A. Wright
Engraver W. F. Hopson
(Plate 02001)

Internet searches reveal a large number of Hopson bookplates are still to be found inside of the front covers of books. The Connecticut State Library in Hartford inserted Hopson bookplates in all of its books starting 1902. The Connecticut bookplate design "bears representations of the Seal of the State, the Fundamental Orders of 1638, the Charter of 1662, the Charter Oak, the first State House in Hartford and the Capitol Building."

Pictured are Hopson's *Books of the Graphic Arts*, and *Walden or Life in the Woods* engravings done for the Bibliophile Society members of 1909. Another of Hopson's engravings was shown in an earlier chapter.

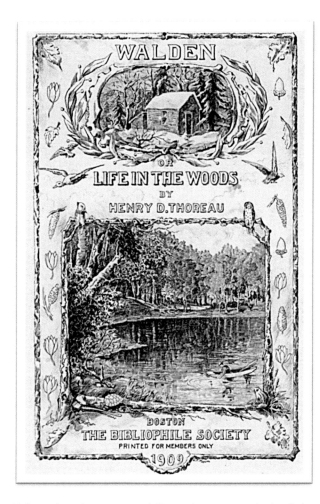

Walden or Life in the Woods
Engraver W. F. Hopson
(Plate 02011)

Occasionally, the Bibliophile Society published editions of selected literary works for its members, including *Walden or Life in the Woods* by **Henry David Thoreau** (1817—1862). Thoreau was "an American author, poet, philosopher, polymath, abolitionist, naturalist, tax resister, development critic, surveyor, historian and leading transcendentalist" according to Thoreau's Wikipedia biographers.

Much of Thoreau's reputation resides on his averseness to the intrusiveness of government in everyday living. He popularized the concept of "civil disobedience", a philosophical perspective that has been used by civil rights, women's rights, right-to-life, and Viet Nam War protestors to justify actions against the government. Thoreau is credited as saying "I ask for, not at once no government, but at once a better government" and "That government is best that governs not at all…"

Although Thoreau's philosophy was admired by Tolstoy, Gandhi, and Martin Luther King, Jr., he regarded "pacifist nonresistance as temptation to passivity."

The Club of Odd Volumes
Engraver Edwin Davis French
(Plate 46047)

The **Club of Odd Volumes** was an English 'Gentleman's Club' with a limited membership in 1883 of 21 members and currently having a membership of 87. Its membership now includes rare and antiquarian book collectors, curators, scholars, printers and typophiles. The Club's library, available only to members, holds about 2,200 titles.

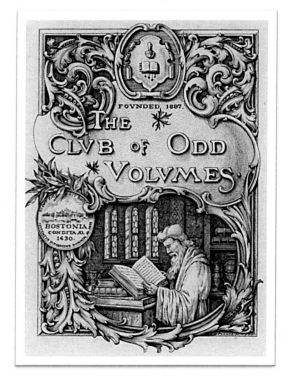

The Grolier Club
Engraver Edwin Davis French
(Plate 46017)

Often called a 'Gentleman's Club', the **Grolier Club** has as its objective "the literary study of the arts pertaining to the production of books..." **Edwin Davis French** (1851—1906) was a member, and engraved over 200 bookplates for American and European collectors, and other members of the Grolier Club.

French, whose engraving was influenced by Albrecht Durer and Charles W. Sherborn, began engraving silver for the Whiting Manufacturing Company and was active in the New York Art Students League and helped found and belonged to the American Fine Arts Society. Among his other interests was the study of artificial languages; he learned Esperanto. The Blackburn Collection includes 210 of French's bookplates together with a copy of *Edwin Davis French: A Memorial His Life, His Art*, copyright by Mary Brainerd French.

Mathew Chaloner Borden (1842—1912) inherited a printing business from his father. Unfortunately, the business failed at first, but with the help of some very highly placed financiers, Mathew was able to build it into the largest cloth printing company in the world while amassing a very large fortune. With success came membership in some very exclusive New York clubs, including the Players Club, Skull and Bones, and the Republican Club.

There were actually two yachts owned by the Borden's, both named *Sovereign*. The first was renamed the Scorpion after it was purchased 1898 by the U.S. Navy for use in the Spanish and American war. The second yacht was also purchased from Borden by the Navy in 1918 for use in the First World War and was renamed the *USS Sovereign*. It was returned by the Navy to the Borden estate in 1919.

The Bookplate Junkie, who at the time he wrote was the Director of the Society of Bookplate Collectors and Designers wrote that the *Sovereign* plate was "designed by Thomas Tryon for the library on board Mr. M.C.D. Bordon's yacht *Sovereign*. {When} the owner objected to the 'crown', Mr. Tryon designed a second plate, slightly differing in some details, and in which an Eagle was substituted for the Crown. The first, or 'Crown' plate, exists only in proof state, and is one of the rarest plates engraved by E. D. French. During the Spanish-American War, the yacht *Sovereign* was purchased by the United States Government and renamed the Scorpion."

Sovereign for M.C. D. Borden Engraver Edwin Davis French 1851--1906
(Plate 46052, 46053)

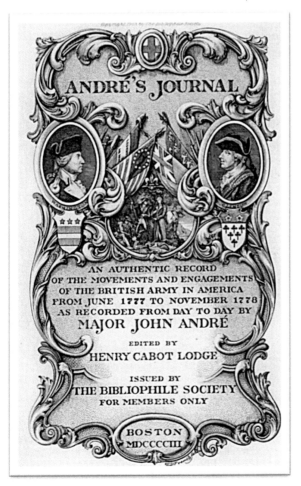

Andre's Journal
Engraver Edwin Davis French
(Plate 49042)

Major John Andre (1750—1780), a British army officer during the American Revolutionary War, helped Benedict Arnold become a traitor. Andre, by all accounts a very personable prisoner, was hanged as a spy when caught in civilian dress. His journal recorded the Operations of the British Army under Lieutenant Generals Sir William Howe and Sir Henry Clinton (1777—1778).

129

Atherton Clark (1826—1882) was a Civil War Army Officer who recruited and commanded the 20th Maine Volunteer Infantry that defended Little Round Top in the Battle of Gettysburg on the second day of the battle.

Atherton Clark
Engraver J. Winfred Spenceley
(Plate 44043)

At the beginning of the battle, Confederate General Lee ordered General Longstreet (commanding Brigadier General Law's forces) to attack. Little Round Top was mostly undefended at the time, but the Union General Chamberlain with 386 officers and men of the 20th Maine regiment and the 83rd Pennsylvania through a clever tactical maneuver successfully repulsed two charges by the Confederates. Almost out of ammunition, Chamberlain ordered a fixed-bayonets charge that won the day and 30 years later a Medal of Honor for Chamberlain. Subsequently, historians credited Lieutenant Holman S. Melcher for initiating the bayonet charge. The 20th Maine under Atherton Clark and the 83rd Pennsylvania thus played a large part in turning the war in favor of the Union.

George Goodrich
Engraver J. Winfred Spenceley
(Plate 44041)

Although **J. Winfred Spenceley** (1865—1908) is regarded as one of the premier bookplate artists of the 20th century, very little biographical data is available about him. He worked in Boston, Massachusetts doing line engraving (as distinguished from etching with a chemical). His bookplates represent a variety of motifs, as emerges in the George Goodrich plate that shows an antiquated Norman medieval English castle with an inset coat of arms. The castle, incidentally, was held by both Royalist and Parliamentary forces during the English Civil War of 1640s, finally brought to ruin by shelling from the "Roaring Meg" mortar in 1646.

Frederick Starr
Engraver J. Winfred Spenceley
(Plate 44042)

Frederick Starr (1858—1933) was an educator and anthropologist who undertook studies of pygmies in Africa and Amerindians in Mexico. Although he taught at the University of Chicago, his studies were not always well received as he was apt to describe his subjects in stereotypical language. His descriptions of the treatment of the Congolese in the Congo Free State by the Austrians, for example, was seen as whitewashing of the brutal treatment of the natives by European whites who were colonists at the time. The themes covered in the Starr plate show the various life experiences of the plate's owner who was a highly traveled anthropologist.

A Painter Etcher
Engraver Charles William Sherborn
(Plate 28001)

Charles William Sherborn (1831—1912) was an English bookplate engraver, painter and etcher, and silver plate engraver who worked in Geneva. He was a regular exhibitor in the Royal Academy in England, and presented a complete set of his paintings, bookplates and etchings to the British Museum. Sherborn's name comes from the castle of the same name built by Sir Walter Raleigh in 1594.

Sherborn worked in Switzerland as a goldsmith designer and engraver, and in London as an engraver for jewelry. As an independent etcher and engraver, he reproduced contemporary portraits and subject paintings, and created many original paintings and bookplates.

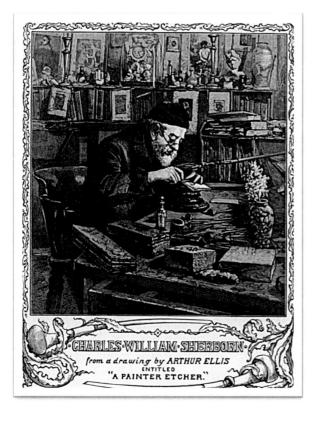

131

Irene Dwen Andrews
Engraver Rockwell Kent
(Plate 11082)

Rockwell Kent (1882—1971) was a painter, writer, illustrator and bookplate designer. Among the books he illustrated were *Moby Dick* by Herman Melville, Voltaire's *Candide*, *The Leaves of Grass* by Walt Whitman and the *Decameron* of Boccaccio.

Kent did dozens of bookplates, among them several for **Irene Dwen Andrews (Pace) (**1892—1962), a writer of books about book and bookplate collecting who also collaborated with her husband on a dictionary of the Tahitian language. Her collection of over 250,000 bookplates is now housed at Yale University Library, Special Collections section.

Rockwell Kent was probably the most sought after and famous of engravers in the early 20th century. His bookplate engravings and other work represent the art deco designs of the period. Because he thought the United States and the Soviet Union ought to be on friendly or at least peaceable terms, Kent became one of the artists targeted by Joseph McCarthy and the House of Un-American Activities Committee.

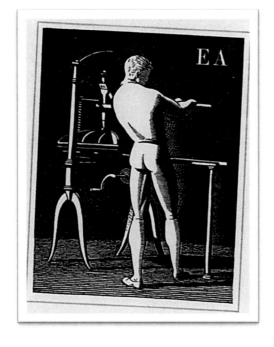

EA
Engraver Rockwell Kent
(Plate 11085)

He donated several hundred of his paintings to the Soviet people, and in 1967 was awarded the Lenin Peace Prize that included funds that he donated to help Vietnamese children. Rockwell Kent was made an honorary member of the Soviet Academy of Fine Arts.

Lucius Lee Hubbard
Engraver Sidney L. Smith
(Plate 13041)

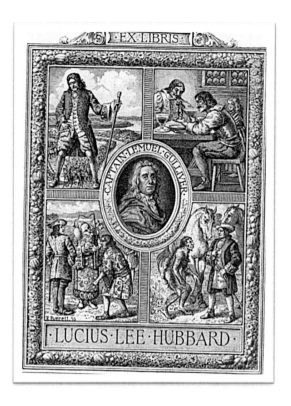

Gardner Teall, writing about **Sidney L. Smith** (1845—1929) in 1921 said "The present century has not found united in the work of a single engraver more varied qualities of excellence…" "…whether it be portraiture, landscape, architecture, allegory, symbolism, heraldic design, or lettering, one does not find a dull line, an insipid conception, inadequate technique, or touch of commonplace".

Wallace Heckman
Engraver Ralph M. Pearson
(Plate 39004)

Ralph Pearson's (1883—1958) bookplates are highly collectible. He was a Southwest artist who was "one of the first American etchers to emphasize formal relations and the key elements of design" according to one art critic.

Pearson studied at the Art Institute of Chicago, and later moved to the southwest where he did most of his work. His etchings are found in the collections of the Library of Congress, the New York Public Library, the Art Institute of Chicago, the Museum of Fine Arts and Columbia University. The plates shown are from copy number 55/250 of *A Portfolio of Original Etched Bookplates* by Ralph M. Pearson published by the American Bookplate Society, Kansas City, 1921.

Wallace Heckman was a Chicago lawyer and supporter of the arts who helped start the Eagle's Nest Art colony, now a part of Southern Illinois University.

133

Irving and Ione Scales
Engraver Ralph Pearson
(Plate 39002)

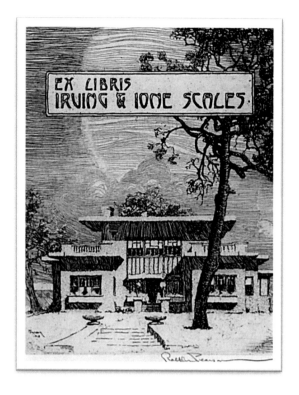

Biographical information was not found for **Irving and Ione Scales**. The 1920s architectural styles of the house with the engraved brushstrokes in the background sky provide an interesting set of contrasts.

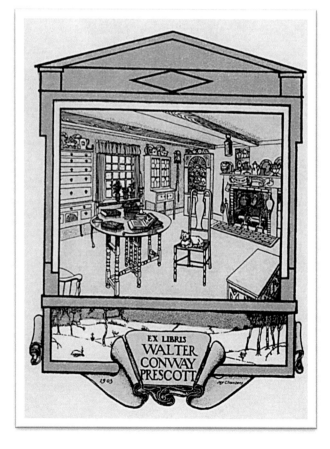

Walter Conway Prescott
Engraver Jay Chambers
(Plate 39058)

Jay Chambers (1878—1929) studied with Howard Pyle at the Drexel Institute where he learned the bookplate trade. He married Laha Whitaker, a former actress, in 1900, and they had a son the next year.

In 1902, Chambers and two associates started a company called Decorative Designers in New York City, where they produced designs for the leading publications of the day. Because he drew human figures well, Chambers became the company's leading portraitist. Whitaker Chambers, their son, became a central character in the spy scandals of the 1950's.

Ruth Thompson Saunders (1901—1952) together with her husband established a print studio in Claremont, California where she designed over a hundred bookplates for libraries and friends. Among those was the Curtis Edmund Avery plate. Several of her plates are held in the collection of Knox College in Galesburg, Illinois, her alma mater. Two of her other plates were for Jack Smith and May Robson, both in the entertainment business.

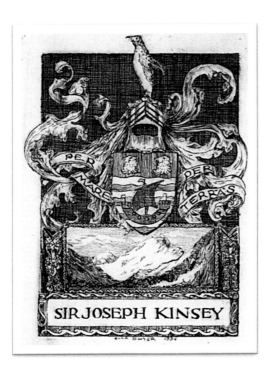

Sir Joseph Kinsey
Engraver Ella Dwyer
(Plate 09008)

Ella Dwyer (1887—1979) was an Australian printmaker and bookplate etcher. She was a foundation member of the Australian Bookplate Club in 1932; her works are held in collections across Australia. George D. Perrottet, another Australian engraver, produced a 2 color linocut for Ella Dwyer.

Joseph James Kinsey (1852—1936) was born in England but immigrated to New Zealand in 1880, where he founded a major shipping company, and from where he supported Antarctic expeditions including that of E. Henry Shackleton.

Walter Conway Prescott
Engraver Fred Thompson
(Plate 29035)

Fred Thompson's (1851—1930) biographical sketch relates that he includes almost an infinite variety of smaller allusions in his plates—ink bottles, quill pens, hour glasses, lamps, cats, dogs, horses, turtles, and flowers.

His studio was on the Charles River, Waltham, Massachusetts where he was an observer of several types of wildlife, including lily-pads and frogs, as shown in the plate below. The hunting camp plate above is one of several commissioned by **Walter Conway Prescott** from a number of engravers that appear throughout the Blackburn Collection of Bookplates.

Mabel Huntington Woods
Engraver Fred Thompson
(Plate 29036)

The frog in **Mabel Huntington Wood's** plate is almost unnoticeable sitting inside the plant. The Latin inscription "Suum cuique. Neum et tuum" means ownership or proprietorship.

Doris Estelle Hight
Engraver Dan Burne Jones
(Plate 03002)

With a little anticipation, two reviewers of **Dan Burne Jones** (1908—1995) bookplate art—**Doris Estelle Hight** and John Baima—observed about the 'national scene' of art, "this great Middle West is possessed of an impetus which is gathering momentum…that will flower into a truly American type of expression, free from the contaminating French influence…" a movement "led by Grant Wood, Thomas Benton and John Stewart Curry" and, they add, Dan Burne Jones. "There is a realism in his barefoot girls and brawny men…" His plates included in the *Annual Bookplate Yearbook* are printed on different colors of paper, adding color to the black inked plate.

Dan Burne Jones studied at the Art Institute of Chicago where he learned lithography, wood block, linocut, wood engraving, and zinc and copper process etching. He had a midwestern background, being born in a coal mining camp in north-central Illinois. Besides bookplate engraving, he taught in several schools and colleges.

S. J. H.
Engraver Sidney Hunt
(Plate 03064)

Although Dan Burne Jones' plates have the imagery of the art deco movement of the 1930s also characteristic of Rockwell Kent, **Sidney Hunt's** (1896—1940) figures have a cubist style made famous by Picasso and Georges Braque.

Many of Hunt's plates were entirely abstract and always interesting insofar as they defied conventions of the day and mirrored the decadence movement in literature represented by the English writer Oscar Wilde and French poet Baudelaire, and artist and engraver Aubrey Beardsley.

137

George David Perrottet
Engraver George D. Perrottet
(Plate 29008)

One of the most accomplished linocut bookplate engravers, **George D. Perrottet** (1890—1971) wrote "Although the process of lino-cutting has been used for book plates for considerable time… they have been but a sort of poor relation to the wood-cut plate. …the medium is capable of broad effects particularly in regard to colour work" … "I use an old letter copying press…ink is applied to the surface of the block with a small roller, the paper place on top, and the impression gained by rubbing the back of the paper with a burnisher or the back of a spoon".

Ella Dwyer
Engraver George D. Perrottet
(Plate 29009)

In some plates, Perrottet used two, three or more blocks, a method reminiscent of Japanese wood block printing. By 1941, Perrottet had completed 162 linocut bookplates. Linocut bookplates are printed from an engraved design using linoleum as the base on which the image is cut.

Arnold Hartman
Engraver J. H. Elwell
(Plate 06043)

The Arnold Hartmann plate is somewhat unique being an engraving of a Chinese Junk with a pagoda in the background and a sampan in the foreground, indicative of the fascination with Oriental art that was appearing in Europe in the late 1800s and early 1900s.

The engraver for the Arnold Hartmann plate was **J.H. Elwell** (1878-1955).

E. Wyllys Andrews IV
Engraver J. W. Jameson
(Plate 05021)

The iconography in the **E. Wyllys Andrews IV** plate shows a humorous rendition of a Mayan stelae.

The first European discovery of Mayan stela was by a Spaniard named Diego Garcia de Placio at Copan, Honduras in 1576. Many of the stelae in Copan are still in their original locations, and can be seen on a casual walk through the Ruinas de Copan.

J. W. Jameson (1882-1939) engraved the E. Wyllys Andrews IV plate.

139

Elizabeth Watson Diamond
Engraver J. W. Jameson
(Plate 05044)

The **Elizabeth Watson Diamond** plate (she and her husband were book and bookplate collectors, and commissioned several plates from a variety of engravers) has an Arab-Persian-Mughal motif reminiscent of *The Rubaiyat of Omar Khayyam.*

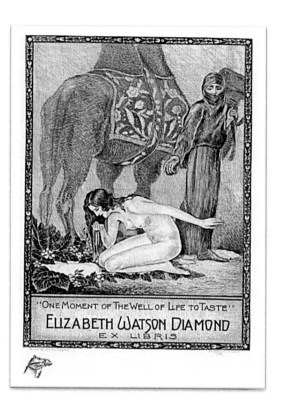

Cornelia Eames Anthony
Engraver J. W. Jameson
(Plate 05015)

The building in the **Cornelia Eames Anthony** (1843-1935) plate has the inscription on the stone that indicates it is the site of the Lincoln-Douglas debates. She was a bookplate collector, and also a collector of Lincoln artifacts and documents. Anthony collected many of Oscar Taylor Blackburn's bookplates that are now housed at the West Chicago Public Library.

Boston Tea Party
Engraver J. H. Elwell
(Plate 06037)

The Boston Tea Party etching is not an ex libris, but **John Hudson Elwell** (1878—1955) created several bookplates during his artistic career, many with a ship or sailboat motif. Paul Revere was a member of the group that threw the tea in the harbor at Boston, and created the original engraving.

Frederick Bonn Fisher
Engraver J. W. Jameson
(Plate 05009)

J. W. Jameson (1882-1939) was an etcher, engraver and illustrator, best known for his ex libris, and was a graduate of the Art Institute of Chicago.

Jameson pursued many motifs in his plates but among them were religious and cultural influences. The religious symbols in the **Frederick Bonn Fisher** plate include a Christian cross, a Buddhist temple, a Moslem mosque, and at the bottom of the plate is a Tibetan prayer wheel.

Jameson generally included on each of his plates a small insignia at the bottom such as the camel head at the bottom of the Elizabeth Watson Diamond plate, the teapot in the Cornelia Eames Anthony plate.

141

Michel Fingesten (1883—1943) infused his ex libris with his artistic expression and a wide variety of subjective interests. Over a thirty year period, he created over two thousand different plates. He received commissions from collectors all over the world, including the two represented here, Irene Dwen Andrews and Elisabeth W. Diamond.

Because he traveled widely, Fingesten's clientele and designs were worldly and adventurous. His themes were Love, Hunger, Death, etc., with a touch of the erotic or cynical. His bookplate society yearbook biographer observes a passionate 'lashing out' at the enemies of humanity that he perceived in the lead up to World War II. Fingesten died in an internment camp near Cosenza, Italy. Among his projects were *Danse Macabre* illustrations of the cycle of war.

Elizabeth W. Diamond
Engraver Michel Fingesten
(Plate 03005)

It's interesting that both J. W. Jameson and Michel Fingesten did Elizabeth Diamond plates that are similar in their design and motif. Diamond was a book collector and with her husband operated a printing business out of her home. She commissioned several plates for herself by artists including Sidney L. Smith, Adrian Feint, Kalban Kubinyi, Sara Eugenia Blake, and Paul Landacre.

A Very Short History of Bookplate Engraving

The bookplate, usually printed on a small 3 x 4 inch paper that is affixed inside the front cover of a book to show ownership, may be construed to be the final stage of a series of literary activities. Authors write books, printers and publishers assemble them, libraries and individuals buy them, and with luck other people read, borrow and return them. To insure their return, bookplates are inserted inside the front cover with the name and identity of the owner.

Before mass production, book ownership was generally the privilege of relatively few wealthy, institutional or religious persons. However, since most books were meant to be widely read, most owners were willing to lend their books to others subject to their being returned. Bookplates were created to assist in the book's return to its owner. A whole industry of bookplate design, engraving and printing was established. In and of themselves, having a personalized bookplate became a mark of distinction, often with a secondary value of expressing an owner's characteristics and sense of personal investment in a book. For many years, the ownership of a bookplate was an expression of social status or of royal lineage and often included a family coat-of-arms in its design. As will be seen in the pages that follow, bookplate design became an artistic expression for both the owner and the designer.

According to Phyllis King writing in the *1951 Year Book of the American Society of Book Plate Collectors and Designers* "The first English bookplate denoting personal ownership was that of Sir Thomas Tresham dated 29 June 1585". Sir Thomas Tresham was a Catholic politician during the Tudor dynasty who helped Henry VIII acquire his fourth wife, Anne of Cleves. In 1557, he was the Grand Pryor of England in the Order of Knights of Hospitallers of St. John of Jerusalem.

As early as forty years after William Caxton introduced the printing press to England in 1476, the first bookplate was created. Caxton himself used a printer's device--a stamp or insignia with his initials surrounded by an elaborated border—in 1478 to identify books he printed.

Among the earliest of German engravers was Albert Durer, also famous as a portrait artist, who may have designed as many as 20 bookplates. Two early woodcut artists who contributed to book and bookplate development were the Elder and Younger Holbeins. Besides woodcuts, Holbein the Younger painted portraits of several members of English royalty during Henry VIII's time, including Henry VIII, Elizabeth I, Jane Seymour, Oliver Cromwell, Sir Thomas Moore, and Sir Henry Wyatt.

Facsimile of the earliest known Book Plate,
made in the year 1480.

Egerton Castle (1859-1920) wrote that bookplates began to appear as early as 1516, and included in his book *English Book-Plates* (1893) a facsimile of a plate given to the University of Cambridge by Sir Nicholas Bacon in 1574. The earliest dated plate found in the Blackburn Collection is a facsimile of a plate with an angel holding a shield showing a goat and having a bottom inscription "Facsimile of the earliest known Book Plate made in the year 1480." As it appears in the facsimile, the plate is in six colors and appears to be printed from a woodcut. (The Bacon bookplate is the only plate included in this book not held in the Blackburn Collection.) It is believed the plate was hand-colored after being printed.

Earliest Known Bookplate
Gift of Brother Hildebrand Brandenburg
of Biberach (Plate 11048)

A colorful figure himself, Egerton Castle was an expert bookplate collector and author. He wrote several novels with his wife, Agnes, and in addition to *English Book-Plates* wrote a history of fencing titled *Schools and Masters of Fencing: From the Middle Ages to the Eighteenth Century*, reprinted in 2003. Castle was a fencer himself and at the age of 50 became the captain of the British epee and sabre teams in the 1908 Olympics.

Three of his written works can be found in Project Gutenberg including *The Light of Scarthy*, a novel in three parts about the love of two women and smuggled gold. Several of Castle's fictional works describe dueling with swords with dramatic clarity.

Egerton Castle
Engraver Unknown
(Plate 10022)

As indicated above, ex libris (a Latin phrase meaning 'from the books of') has been placed in books for about 400 years to facilitate ownership, identification and return of books. Castle wrote "Furthermore, from the thickly pressing ranks of armorial labels telling of wealthy and otherwise excellent book-owners who, however, may be utterly unknown to Biography, there will occasionally shine forth the book-plate of some famous man or woman—long since dust".

Many of the bookplates are signed either by their owners or by the designers and engravers. The signature of Egerton Castle was included in the Blackburn Collection as a stand-alone item; however many original and facsimile signatures are found on the bookplates themselves.

Even though the initial creation of bookplates began with a simple inscription of the owner's name, bookplates also helped record the book's provenance (ownership over generations of a book's life) and libraries to which the book belonged. Sometimes, several bookplates are found in the same book identifying transfer of ownership. This is particularly the case where private libraries are sold, and new owners retain the original plate while also inserting their own.

Egerton Castle's 'Bacon'
Engraver Nicholas Bacon
(Plate 50200)

Over the years, a substantial literature has grown up around the creation and collection of bookplates. Three source books came with the Blackburn Collection, Egerton Castle's *English Bookplates* (1893), Charles Dexter Allen's *American Book Plates* (1894), and Esther Griffin White's *Indiana Bookplates* (1910).

Each of these authors was expert in the history of bookplate design and collection, and their books themselves are now collector's items. The Collection also included ten editions of the *Year Books* published by the *American Society of Bookplate Collectors and Designers*. Some estimates indicate that over a million unique bookplates have been designed and printed over the years.

One of the earliest great English libraries was that of **Sir Thomas Browne** (1605—1682), who was said to have known five languages—French, Italian, Spanish, Dutch and Danish—and has been identified as the first source for over 800 English words.

Browne's collection, now part of the British Library, included books written in Greek, Hebrew and Latin and had about 1500 titles. The subjects covered were history, geography, philology, anatomy, philosophy, theology, cartography, embryology, medicine, cosmography, ornithology, mineralogy, zoology, travel, law, mathematics, geometry, literature, astronomy, chemistry, astrology alchemy, physiognomy, and the Kabbalah. The item identified as plate 26025, a handwritten note, is from Sir Thomas Browne's library and was created about 1655.

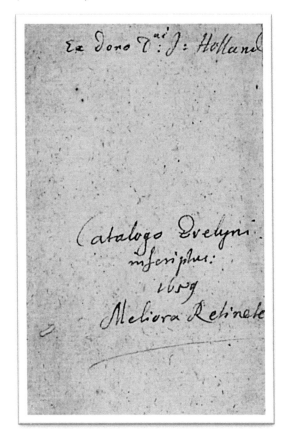

-Great libraries are still the pride of their owners; many are assembled by governments, the most complete being the Library of Congress and the British libraries. Extensive libraries are found in major universities such as Harvard and Yale and in research universities whose accreditation and ability to attract research scholars and research funds is determined in part by the extensiveness of their libraries. Yale University among others has an immense collection of bookplates in its holdings and sponsors a internet page that is available for research purposes.

Private individuals, who collect books for their personal libraries, invest a great amount of time and funds for caring for antiquarian and modern books. Many of the inscriptions found on bookplates extoll the virtues of books and libraries, an activity especially true in earlier times. John Adams' library was said to contain 3,000 volumes, and Benjamin Franklin had 4,726 titles in his library. These libraries were not large by today's measure, but in their time they were considered great libraries.

INDEX
Alphabetical by Engraver

Spenceley, J.Winfred

Atherton Clark	130	44043
George Goodrich	130	44041
Frederick Starr	131	44042

Thompson, Fred

Walter Conway Prescott	136	29035
Mabel Huntington Woods	138	29036

Tice, Clara

Bruno's Garret	106	33062
Two Girls Peacock	107	33054
Three Girls In A Fountain	107	33057

Tiffany And Co.

Henry W. Taft	67	29022

Unknown

Egerton Castle	144	10022
Catalogo Evelyni	146	26025
Winston Churchill	6	36035
Richard De Gylpyn	11	33046
St. Giles Church at Pontefract photo	12	50117
Thomas Blackburn, Esq. Of Hale Near Warrington, Lancashire	13	40023
John Blackburn	14	17022
W. Blackburn	14	40024
John Blackburn Esq. Of Hale	15	40022
Andrew Blackburn	15	40026
Bibliotheca Elizabethana Apud Blackburn In Com:Lane	16	40025
Wm. Blackburn M.D.	16	40028
Ambrose Holbech Of Mollington	17	18050
William Norcliffe Of The Inner Temple London	18	18052
Gostlet Harington Of Marshfield In The County Of Cloucester	18	18051
William Fitzroy, Duke Of Cleveland	19	18132
Bruce Of Ampthill	19	41060
Sir Thomas Hanmer Of Hanmer	20	41063
Deburgh Earl Of Clanricarde	20	41054
Dashwood, Lord Le Despencer	21	41051
Lord Archibald Campbell, 5th Earl of Argyle	22	36002
Walter Raleigh, Divine	22	26005
Lord Napier	23	36013
Thomas Fytton Armstrong	24	26053
Lord Henry Grey, 11th Duke of Kent	24	36017
Sir Robert Walpole	25	36010
Lord And Lieutenant General Cornwallis	25	36032
Charlotte Sophia, Queen Of George Iii	26	36027
Princess Sophia, Daughter Of George Iii	26	36028
Arthur Wellesley	27	36001
General Wyndham	28	40015
Spencer Perceval, Prime Minister For George IV	28	36014
Bejamin Disraeli	29	36039
William Ewart Gladstone	29	36036
William Ewart Gladstone	30	36037
Archduke Maximilian	30	36020
Archduke Maximilian And Queen Charlotte Of Belgium	30	36022
Execution of Maximilian News Photo	31	36023
Albert, Prince Of Wales	31	18125
George Frederick Ernest Albe	32	36030
Thomas Wyatt	35	12056

David Hume	36	25005
Thomas Campbell	36	33038
Adam Smith	36	25042
John Hall Stevenson	37	25029
William Cowper	37	33047
Edward Gibbon	37	25018
Anna Damer	38	23016
Mary Berry	38	23008
Thomas Pennant	39	25053
W.H. Ireland	39	26038
Newstead Abby, Home Of Lord Byron	39	25020
Thomas Carlyle	40	26010
Thomas Hood	40	33042
Anthony Trollope	41	25023
Sir Richard Burton	41	26014
George Meredith	42	26017
Algernon Charles Swinburne	42	33040
Josepth B. Priestly	43	26035
Thomas Burke	43	25028
Margot Tennant, Lady Asquith	44	23005
Alfred, Lord Tennyson	44	33018
Thomas Hardy	44	26047
Rudyard Kipling	45	26056
Charles Dickens Commemorative Stamp	48	38023
Charles Dickens	48	38022
Charles Kingsley	48	25017
Justin Mccarthy	50	25008
E. Temple Thurston	50	25056
Enoch Arnold Bennett	51	26007
William Penn	53	27005
William Byrd Of Westover	54	20064
George Washington	54	20001
George Washington	55	20002
Bushrod Washington	55	20037
John Adams	58	20028
John Adams	57	20029
Thomas Jefferson	58	20009
Marquis De La Fayette	59	20039
James Monroe	59	20022
John Quincy Adams	60	20023
John Quincy Adams	60	20024
Philip Schuyler	61	40009
Alexander Hamilton	61	20036
Daniel Webster	62	27003
Abraham Lincoln	62	20013
Mary Todd Lincoln	63	20014
Edward Everett	63	24041
William Tecmseh Sherman	64	40001
Harriet Beecher Stowe	64	24043
William Mckinley	65	20011
Theodore Roosevelt	65	20012
Theodore Roosevelt	66	20031
Ellen Axson Wilson	67	24050
Woodrow Wilson	68	20020
Herbert Hoover	69	20016